Compulsive gamblers

Longman Applied Psychology
General Editor: Philip Feldman

The social creation of mental illness
Raymond Cochrane

Compulsive gamblers
Mark G. Dickerson

Psychological aspects of pregnancy
Anthony Reading

Forthcoming:
Biofeedback in practice
Douglas Carroll

Chemical control of behaviour
Steven Cooper

Clinical psychology of the elderly
A. D. M. Davies and A. G. Crisp

Drink and drinking problems
Clive Eastman

Behavioural medicine
P. G. Harvey and B. Dodd

Methods of changing behaviour
Andree Liddell

The schizophrenias
M. J. Birchwood, P. Green and M. C. Preston

Fears and anxieties
D. C. Rowan and C. Eayrs

Institutional care and rehabilitation
Geoffrey Shepherd

Compulsive gamblers

Mark G. Dickerson

Longman
London and New York

Longman Group Limited
Longman House, Burnt Mill, Harlow
Essex CM20 2JE, England
Associated companies throughout the world

*Published in the United States of America
by Longman Inc., New York*

© Longman Group Limited 1984

First published 1984

British Library Cataloguing in Publication Data
Dickerson, Mark G.
   Compulsive gamblers. – (Longman applied psychology)
   1. Gambling
   I. Title
   157'7   HV6722

   ISBN 0-582-29606-4

Library of Congress Cataloging in Publication Data
Dickerson, Mark G.
   Compulsive gamblers.
   (Longman applied psychology)
   Bibliography: p.
   Includes index.
1. Gamblers – Psychology.   2. Gamblers – United States.
3. Compulsive behavior. I. Title. II. Series.
HV6710.D52 1984 362.2'9 82-24891
ISBN 0-582-29606-4

Set in 9½/11 pt Linotron 202 Times
Printed in Hong Kong by
Astros Printing Ltd.

Contents

For my parents
Ursula and Dick

Editor's preface

In most areas of applied psychology there is no shortage of hardback textbooks many hundreds of pages in length. They give a broad coverage of the total field but rarely in sufficient detail in any one topic area for undergraduates, particularly honours students. This is even more true for trainees and professionals in such areas as clinical psychology.

The Longman Applied Psychology series consists of authoritative short books each concerned with a specific aspect of applied psychology. The brief given to the authors of this series was to describe the current state of knowledge in the area, how that knowledge is applied to the solution of practical problems and what new developments of real-life relevance may be expected in the near future. The twelve books which have been commissioned so far are concerned mainly with clinical psychology, defined very broadly. Topics range from gambling to ageing and from the chemical control of behaviour to social factors in mental illness.

The books go into sufficient depth for the needs of students at all levels and professionals yet remain well within the grasp of the interested general reader. A number of groups will find their educational and professional needs or their personal interests met by this series: Professional psychologists and those in training (clinical, educational, occupational, etc.); psychology undergraduates; undergraduate students in other disciplines which include aspects of applied psychology (e.g. social administration, sociology, management, and particularly medicine); professionals and trainee professionals in fields outside psychology, but which draw on applications of psychology (doctors of all kinds, particularly psychiatrists and general practitioners, social workers, nurses, particularly psychiatric nurses, counsellors – such as school, vocational and marital – and personnel managers).

Finally, members of the general public who have been introduced to a particular topic by the increasing number of well-informed and well-presented newspaper articles and television programmes will be able to follow it up and pursue it in more depth.

Philip Feldman

Acknowledgements

I am indebted to innumerable men and women who over the last twelve years or so have shared with me their experiences of gambling. Many of them I have met in the context of Gamblers Anonymous meetings in the UK and in Australia. The GA organisation itself has generously aided me in research projects and I am particularly grateful to two of their officers, Gerry and Jean. Gordon Moody, Emmanuel Moran and Bob Custer have encouraged my continued interest in the topic. Many other friends and colleagues have shared my enthusiasm for the subject and Chris Williams, Ian Brown and Phil Wookey have helped me clarify and develop my ideas; the inconsistencies and faults that remain are mine alone. I am most grateful to those who read and commented upon earlier drafts of the text, Olivia Dickerson, Tania Dziadosz, Martin Therkelsen and Kathy Leary. Finally I should like to express my gratitude to Sue Poultney, Robyn Creech and Jess Giddings for the care given in the preparation of the manuscript.

Chapter 1

Introduction

'Fred was not a gambler: he had not that specific disease in
which the suspension of the whole nervous energy on a chance
or risk becomes as necessary as the dram to the drunkard;'
(Of Fred Vincy when seeking additional funds to repay an
outstanding gambling debt.)

George Eliot *Middlemarch* (1871)

Writing about gambling is almost as hazardous as writing
about sex; both topics are rarely discussed without moral
overtones. Most readers commonly assume that the writer
is either for or against it. Some authors of gambling tracts,
perhaps realising this problem and maybe even wishing to
capitalise on the reader's prejudices, have clearly sig-
nalled their intention in their titles e.g. 'Gambling: a
positive view' (Campbell 1976) and *The Facts about the
'Money Factories'* (Moody 1972).

The title of Compulsive Gamblers, together with the
information that the author is a clinician who has worked
closely with Gamblers Anonymous (GA), might suggest
that this work is in support of an anti-gambling lobby.
Rather than give an outright denial, suffice it to say that
one would have to be something of a dullard not to accept
that gambling, whether legalised or not, will always be an
integral part of most cultures and societies. Instead of
morals, the message here is one of interest and enthusiasm
for an intriguing and little-understood aspect of human

behaviour that is associated with the public appearance of a billion-dollar business whenever it is legalised.

Most writings about gambling start out with a definition or two. In common parlance 'gambling' might refer to anything from riding a bike with 'no hands', to buying and selling shares, to flipping a coin. Some authors (e.g. Perkins 1950) give definitions such as:

1 Exchange of money which takes place without any equivalent value, material or personal
2 Possession of money determined solely by chance
3 Winner's gain solely by loss of losers
4 The risk taken is avoidable.

This is an intellectual nicety perhaps but not of great assistance with the present task. As most people have gambled in one way or another, readers can draw upon their own experience. Throughout this book the main focus of our attention will be upon the well-known forms of commercialised gambling; horse- and dog-race betting, casino gaming, poker-machine playing and, to a lesser extent, pools, bingo and lotteries.

The definition of 'compulsive gambler' is however a matter of theoretical importance and some detailed consideration is given to this later in the book (see Ch. 4 and 5). At this stage it is sufficient to assume that compulsive gamblers are people (usually but not invariably men) who approach treatment or helping agencies with statements to the effect that they cannot control their urge to gamble, that they want to stop or reduce their gambling. When questioned further they commonly describe a series of monetary, marital, employment and even legal problems associated with or caused by their gambling. Such people are the focus of this book. The majority of the text is concerned to provide a detailed description of the way they gamble (Ch. 4), to review critically theoretical explanations of why they persist in gambling when losing, often for many years (Ch. 5), and finally to evaluate the methods that have been used to help them stop or regain control of their gambling (Ch. 6).

Although descriptions of the emperors Nero and Claudius suggest that the history of compulsive gamblers is long, the first papers on the topic appeared in the scientific journals at the beginning of this century. Most of the early interest was shown by psychoanalysts, notably Bergler (1957) who treated sixty compulsive gamblers. Indeed, most of the literature to date has been based on people who have sought help, most commonly from psychiatric care or from the self-help organisation, Gamblers Anonymous, which was founded in 1957. The literature has emphasised the concepts of 'illness' and 'treatment', although recent contributions by sociologists (e.g. Oldman 1978) have provided alternative perspectives.

It is generally agreed (Bolen 1974; Custer 1982; Greenberg 1980) that compulsive gamblers have been the subject of little consistent and methodologically sound research. In the past the medical profession has been ambivalent about providing treatment for gamblers (e.g. editorial of the *British Medical Journal* 1968). A general practitioner was reported by a GA member to have reacted to his story with, 'But I garden a lot, am I a compulsive gardener?' However, at the present time three states in the US Maryland, Connecticut and New York, have enacted legislation to establish state-funded treatment programmes for gamblers seeking help with their problems.

The present rule-of-thumb used to estimate the number of compulsive gamblers is a little under 1 per cent of the adult male population (*c.* 1.1 million in the US). In addition there is some evidence to suggest that each compulsive gambler adversely affects at least ten other people (Politzer & Morrow 1980). The schema from Custer (1982) (Fig. 1) illustrates the stages through which the gambler is supposed to pass during the development of, and recovery from, the problem of 'pathological gambling'. The latter is listed under 'disorders of impulse' as a diagnostic category included in the American Psychiatric Association's latest classification of mental disorders,

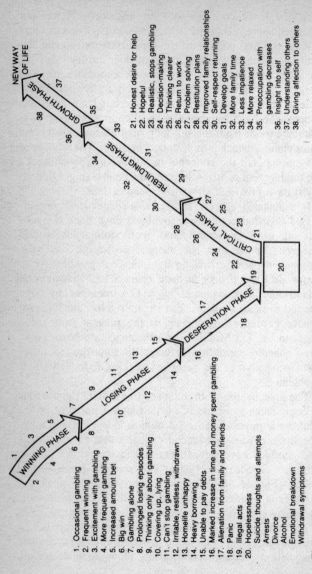

Fig. 1 The stages of pathological gambling and recovery (*Source:* Adapted from Custer 1982)

DSM-III (1980). To suggest that this represents the latest production in the manufacture of mental illness (Szasz 1961) or in the medicalisation of yet another social problem (Roman 1980) might needlessly belittle the genuine advances in the availability of help for gamblers with problems that have been pioneered by Bob Custer over many years in the United States.

It is more productive for this discussion to note the similarity between the schema for pathological gambling and that produced over a quarter of a century ago by Jellinek (1952) describing the stages in the disease model of alcoholism which subsequent research has failed to substantiate. This piece of history should serve as a helpful warning about the present state of the art concerning compulsive gamblers. However, useful parallels may be drawn with more recent advances in the study and treatment of alcoholism. This has been done from time to time throughout the book. One development may be helpfully considered at this point; the move away from the disease model of alcoholism has been associated with the development of a body of knowledge about all drinkers so that the so-called 'sick' or alcoholic drinker no longer appears so deviant but may even be indistinguishable from social drinkers, except in terms of the amount of alcohol consumed (Marlatt 1979).

As far as compulsive gamblers are concerned almost all the publications to date have been based on information derived from gamblers seeking help or attending GA. Such gamblers have often been compared with the 'social gambler' who , it has been assumed, gambles occasionally, once a week or less. Therefore, not surprisingly, those gamblers who have sought help appear exceedingly deviant and have attracted the labels of 'pathological' and 'compulsive'.

One of the primary objectives of this book is to piece together, from a variety of sources, information about regular or high-frequency gamblers as an alternative and preferable perspective in which to assess compulsive gamblers. This has been done in Chapter 4 where it is concluded that, given our present stage of knowledge, the compulsive gambler is sometimes distinguishable from other regular or high-frequency gamblers only by the amount of money he or she loses.

This is not to say that gamblers who seek help do not have genuinely serious and complex problems; they most certainly do and some of the dimensions of these problems will be encountered later in the book. Another conclusion drawn from the collation of empirical data on regular gamblers is to support the recent inclusion of compulsive gambling in the general category of addictive behaviours, along with smoking, overeating, substance abuse and excessive alcohol drinking (Marlatt 1979; Miller 1980).

The implications for theory, treatment, future research and social policy that flow from these conclusions provide important themes in the subsequent chapters. However, before we focus our attention on men and women who gamble frequently there is a need to establish an overall perspective on gambling activities and to review some of the general theories that have been advanced to explain why most human beings participate in some form of gambling.

Chapter 2

Historical and contemporary perspectives

This chapter describes how over the centuries various forms of gambling have developed up until the present day when many countries have legalised gambling in some form or other. The information on this topic is potentially enormous. The objective here is limited to providing the reader with a sketch of the gambling scene generally as a context in which to consider the more detailed accounts of compulsive gamblers.

Historical aspects

The history of gambling is long, varied and entertaining; here it is possible only to touch on a few details (for a history of gambling see, for example, Jones 1973). The origins are assumed to be found some 3,000 years BC when Egyptian astragals, the early bone precursors of dice, were used to predict the future. Gambling was an integral part of the mythology of Egypt, with Mercury playing at the tables of the Moon and winning a part of her illuminations – five days which were added to the 360 days in the year and celebrated as the birthdays of the gods. The earliest manuscripts found in India provide reports of heavy gambling on dice and chariot racing as a part of civilised society. Further east in Japan and China some social decisions or policies were determined by the outcome of complex games such as Go and Wei Kei; gambling for money or property was usually associated with simpler and quicker games such as drawing lots.

Accounts of Greek and Roman mythology and history indicate that in both cultures gambling played a significant part in the lives of both the rich and powerful and the common citizen. The emperors Claudius, Nero and Caligula were all reputed to gamble frequently with large sums of money. A Roman tavern sign advertising gambling and food, excavated by archaeologists, indicated that participation in gambling was widespread among the population. Cheating, too, has been confirmed by archaeological finds of weighted dice. Gambling may have contributed to the downfall of German tribal leaders at the hands of Roman invaders. Tacitus reported: 'Under the influence of uncontrollable ecstasy the players gambled their wives, their children and ultimately themselves into captivity.'

Dice-playing has probably the longest history of the forms of gambling available today. Betting on horse and dog races is today one of the most popular forms of gambling but its name 'the sport of kings' indicates that originally it was not an activity in which the ordinary citizen could engage. In the United Kingdom during the twelfth and thirteenth centuries there was little organised horse-racing. The oldest flat race is the Chester Cup, first run in 1512, but it was not until the efforts of James I (1603–25) that spectators were deliberately encouraged. A racing calendar was begun and stables established at Newmarket. The involvement of the Royal family with horse-racing continued with Queen Anne inaugurating the first Royal Ascot in 1711. The world's most famous race, the Derby, was first run in 1780 and the Grand National in 1839. The Kentucky Derby (1875) in the United States, the Queen's Plate (1860) in Canada, and the Melbourne Cup (1830) in Australia support the view that horseracing was generally popular and represented the most readily available opportunity for people to gamble. On-course betting was the one form that was exempt from Charles

II's Act (1745) prohibiting gambling in public. Although this may have resulted in a reduction in the gaming in taverns and bars it lead to the founding of private card-playing clubs some of which in the following century became, and remain today, famous for their association with the rich, royal and powerful who gamble: clubs such as White's and Crockford's.

Lotteries became increasingly popular in England and Europe from the sixteenth century onwards when Elizabeth I with a first prize of £5,000 raised almost £200,000 which was used to finance the repairs of harbours and coastal fortifications. Despite their contemporary trappings the basic form of lotteries has remained virtually unchanged. Two other important forms of gambling have their origins in the work of two inventors, Blaise Pascal and Charles Fey. Pascal, an eighteenth-century mathematician, is credited with the development of the final version of the roulette wheel from three earlier simpler versions: the 'hoca' with three zeros used by Louis IV, the odds and evens wheel, and 'boule' which had a static numbered wheel around the rim of which the ball was spun. Some 150 years later, in 1895, Charles Fey of the United States invented the *poker-machine. Neither inventor in their wildest dreams could have imagined the sums of money that would change hands as a result of their spinning wheels and cylinders. Today the poker-machine, the roulette wheel and betting on horse and dog races represent the three most popular forms of gambling.

Famous names and tall stories

Roulette was especially identified with the gaming rooms of Monte Carlo which until the birth of Las Vegas was a household name, with connotations of the very rich of all nationalities winning or, more usually, losing heavily, and

---

* Commonly known in the UK as one-armed bandits or gaming machines.

occasionally committing an 'honourable' suicide. Various gambling meccas have come and gone but Baden-Baden in West Germany survives as the oldest casino. Las Vegas, London, Paris, Deauville, Cannes, Rome, Venice, San Remo, Salzburg have all attracted the famous names in gambling. These include the 'amateurs' such as the Duke of Wellington, George Washington, the Earl of Sandwich, Benjamin Disraeli, Dostoevsky, Beau Brummel, the Aga Khan and Edward VII. Although 'professional' gamblers such as Nick the Greek (Montreal), Ferencz (France), Hughie Rowan (UK), John 'bet-a-million' Gates (Chicago) and Don Scott (Australia) have achieved a degree of fame, many experienced extreme fluctuations between poverty and riches throughout their gambling careers. Their skills, particularly in regard to casino card games, have been poorly appreciated by casino operators who either view them with ambivalence or ban them from their tables. In the late nineteenth century Zographos was one such card player who, it was claimed, could remember every card played from a baccarat shoe – 312 cards in all.

Hollywood has often been linked with gambling and Bolen (1974) recalls the story of Groucho Marx who came to see an MGM executive dressed in jockey's racing silks with the explanation, 'This is the only way you can get to see a producer these days.' In a typical movie-style story the amateurs, Jack Warner, Darryl Zanuck and Bob Bennett, were reputed in 1957 to have taken over a quarter of a million pounds from the professionals, the Greek Syndicate.

For losers to hit the headlines the sums lost tend to be larger. If Emperor Nero with £21,000 (*$40,000) on a single roll of the dice set the trend then perhaps Kitty Milinaire in 1978 in the UK remains a record-holder with losses of some £3 million (about $5.5 million) in less than three years. When all cash and possessions were lost the

* Dollars used throughout are based on a rough estimate of £1 = $2.

Chinese were reputed to stake, and sometimes lose, their ears. Immediately after the earthquake in London in 1750 people were betting on whether it was indeed an earth tremor or an explosion at a local powder factory. In 1844 in evidence to a Parliamentary Select Committee on gambling it was recorded that one wager hung upon the outcome of a person's ability to jump over a table backwards. Certainly it seems that men and women have bet upon almost any future outcome – the length of lives or governments, the sex of a new royal child or whether the sharks or the rescue boat will first reach a swimming sailor. In the latter, so the story goes, when the boat recovered the man minus his legs it was deemed that the greater portion had been saved and the winners were those who had backed the boat.

Cultural and religious perspectives

Certain cultural differences in gambling activities exist today; dice has never been a favourite in the UK but in Thailand may be interspersed between every shot in a round of golf. However, it is perhaps questionable whether any nation outside of the Third World has not at some moment of self-analysis perceived itself as a 'nation of gamblers'. Certainly this is true of the United States, Australia and the United Kingdom as each country considers, and takes, steps in the direction of the legalisation of all forms of gambling. In the past, Balinese and Chinese cultures have been strongly associated with gambling but in neither was gambling as fully integrated into the social system as in that of the American Indians (Kroeber 1948). For those tribes living north of the Rio Grande there were inter-village gambling contests, not just to win the stakes but to establish that the gods were on one's side, for example in preparation for war. Thus in the languages of these people gambling was often described in the same phrases used for warfare and hunting.

Where gambling is not so integrated in a society condemnation is often advanced by religious leaders. In nineteenth-century England the view of the National Anti-Gambling League was of 'a nation impregnated with a deadly virus' and the winning entry for a hymn composition competition organised by the League in 1905 was entitled 'A Leprosy is O'er the Land'. The disease metaphor was used to 'explain' the dangers of the working people emulating the gambling behaviour of the upper classes.

Some contemporary religious views were summarised in the Rothschild Report (HMSO 1978). Certainly there is a range of views both within and between Christian churches; for example, for the Roman Catholic gambling is not inherently wrong while the Methodist Church states that gambling conflicts with certain fundamental principles, such as its appeal to luck rather than to the law of God. Gambling is also forbidden for the strict Muslim and Sikh. Buddhist views of gambling are expressed in terms of its harmful consequences and impedence of spiritual growth. Rivkind (in Adler & Goleman 1969) noted that folklore and rabbinical sermons in Europe from the fifteenth century onwards expressed a concern for gambling as a peculiarly Jewish problem. However, today many orthodox Jews would see gambling in moderation as quite acceptable.

Moral ambivalence

One theme that may usefully be drawn out from a history of gambling is that of ambivalence. It is rare for a society or an individual to consistently hold firm views either for or against gambling. In the past it has been common for religious views to oppose gambling and yet lotteries and raffles were often spared the reformer's sword, to remain a source of income for many churches. In Nevada, with a large percentage of its congregation employed in the gambling industry the Mormon Church needs must avoid moralising on the matter. Often ambivalence has appeared in the guise of paternalism: gambling as acceptable for the rich and educated but not for the working person. Or even paternalism directed at the rich minority – in the UK an individual's losses in the casino cannot be amalgamated into a single cheque; each cheque written must be processed by his or her bank (the objective being to ensure that the banker knows that the gambler lost more than he or she intended).

The history of legislation for and against gambling serves as a barometer of the swings in public opinion. This is well illustrated in the state of Nevada;

1861: Nye as governor: gambling operations a felony and betting a misdemeanor.

1864: Statehood: 1861 Act repealed; gambling legal but barred from the front room of the first floor of any building.

1909: Prohibition of all gambling mainly as a result of the women's temperance movement.

1911: Some card games legal.

1913: All gambling illegal.

1931: Legalisation of all forms of gambling.

As a final point, ambivalence also characterises the relationship between gambler and bookie, or gambler and casino employee, which is commonly described in terms of love-hate, friend-enemy. The regulars are 'good customers' to their face but 'mug-punters' behind their backs. Winners are good news for a casino provided that they have been lucky rather than skilful. Thus while a Royal Commission may commend to the gambler counting systems in blackjack, in the reality of the casino pit the 'counter' is implicitly warned off, or in Las Vegas publicly barred from all other casinos.

Contemporary aspects of gambling

Gambling in the form of lotteries, football pools, and on- and off-course betting on horse and dog races is available in most countries outside the Third World and is a major industry in the United Kingdom, Europe, Australia and the United States – where there is now some form of legalised gambling in forty-six of the fifty states. The aim in this section is to establish a broad over-view of present-day gambling so that later detailed discussion and analysis of compulsive gamblers may be seen in perspective. A contemporary international review of gambling is not available. Here the aim is restricted to a description of the various forms of gambling, the legalisation of gambling, its popularity and a general description of the amounts spent by individuals on gambling.

Forms of gambling

The commonest forms of gambling are given in Table 2.1. The differential popularity of these main forms cannot be generalised from these data derived from the Rothschild Report (HMSO 1978). In the UK, lotteries and poker-machines are subject to a variety of restrictions. Where lotteries, poker-machines and off-course betting are equally available, as for example in the state of New South Wales, Australia, official taxation revenue figures (Australian Bureau of Statistics 1981) suggest that poker-machines generate the greatest volume of money staked and lost. Whenever casinos, off-course betting on horse

Table 2.1 Gambling in the United Kingdom

	Popularity*	% Paid back in winnings
Casinos	57	97.5
Off-course betting	26	81
Poker machines	6	70
Bingo	4	95
On-Course betting	4	88
Football pools	3	30

* As a % of the total money staked.
(*Source*: HMSO 1978.)

Table 2.2 Casino games

	Banker's edge %	Frequency of play (mins)	Popularity*
American roulette	1.4–2.7	0.75	55
Blackjack	at least 0.6	2–3	19
Punto banco	1.25	2–3	14
French roulette	1.4–2.7	1.5–2	5
Craps	1.4–5.6	1.5–2	3
Baccarat banque	0.9–1.5	2–3	3

* As a % of the total money staked.
(*Source*: HMSO 1978.)

and dog races and poker-machines are all easily available to the general public they tend far to outstrip in
popularity (defined in terms of total money staked) any
other forms of gambling.

Further subdivision within the main forms of gambling
suggests that about 80 per cent of money staked off-course
is placed on horseracing. Certainly, throughout Europe,
the United States and Australia the popularity of horse-
race betting is likely to exceed any other racing whether
dogs, trotting, athletics, motor cycling, etc., although
these too remain the focus of some betting. The differential popularity of the main casino games illustrated in
Table 2.2 may well withstand generalisation to casinos
internationally, except that craps may be more popular in
the United States.

Other forms of gambling can generate an enormous list.
It is sufficient to note that card games, especially poker,
may be the focus for gambling, that the illegal 'numbers'
form of lottery can be an integral part of some ghetto com-
munities in the US (Joyce 1975) and that there is a variety
of games that have an ethnic minority interest from cock-
fighting to mahjong and from 'two-up' to 'spot the ball'!

Legalisation of gambling

Most developed countries have gone some way down the

road toward the legalisation of all forms of gambling. In this respect, with the obvious exception of Nevada, the United States lags somewhat behind Europe and Australia as it continues to decide on how much and what forms of gambling should be generally available. The US Commission on the Review of the National Policy Toward Gambling (1976) was able to draw on the experience of countries such as the United Kingdom in assessing the likely effects of legalisation. In addressing the question of crime, the 1968 amendments to the United Kingdom laws dealing with the control of casinos in particular were explicitly concerned both to limit their number and to regulate their operations in a way that would eliminate the growing criminal involvement in this form of gambling. This experience may be similar to the initial Nevada legislation in 1931 which also was associated with an infiltration of criminal resources and manpower transferred from the bootleg liquor trade.

Despite these apparent similarities in the initial effects of legalising casinos Skolnick (1978), in a comprehensive and stimulating study of the Nevada legislation, highlighted what he felt was a crucial difference between the US and UK approaches. In the United States the characteristic motive has been revenue production – thus, in the extreme, Nevada's economic survival depends on gambling revenue where it is the single largest industry, employing about one-third of the workforce. However, in the UK, gambling, perhaps especially casino gaming, is still viewed as something of a social problem to be controlled, rather than condoned, by legislation. It is therefore the responsibility of the Home Office rather than the Treasury. Skolnick analysed the complexity of the problem of controlling casino gaming and in so doing perhaps provided some understanding of why the UK Gaming Board had such draconian powers – the most autocratic institution since the Star Chamber, he suggested. Given the enormous sums of money involved in casino gaming and the almost impossible task of accurately monitoring cash flow it seems likely that the criminal underworld will continue to seek involvement in this form of gambling. However, present evidence suggests that this involvement can be prevented or reduced to an acceptable level by careful legislation and the implementation of powers of regulation and monitoring.

The legalisation of off-course betting illustrates some of the difficulties of generalizing from one country to another. In the UK prior to the 1960 Act the street 'bookie' was pretty much an accepted part of society; certainly his activities were not viewed as criminal. The Betting and Gaming Act 1960 in some senses confirmed this view and merely facilitated business by permitting offices to be opened. The need for illegal bookmaking virtually disappeared and this has remained so for over twenty years. In the US, however, state-run off-course betting was introduced in competition with illegal bookies but failed to provide equally good facilities or credit availability and thus the police opinion presented to the 1976 Commission was that the new legislation had actually increased the illegal bookies' trade by generating more customers. In the past, prohibition of gambling commonly led only to driving it underground. Certainly, in the US one of the pressures generating the trend towards legalisation is that laws against gambling are massively violated and that illegal gambling, besides being enormously demanding of manpower in its elimination, may be the largest single component in police corruption (Arcuri 1979).

The fear that legalisation of gambling would lead to greater numbers of people participating has been commonly expressed in debates for and against changes in the law. From the experience of various countries it seems likely that where the opportunity to participate in a particular form of gambling already existed, albeit illegally, then the end of prohibition had little impact on the percentage of the population who subsequently gambled, e.g. participation in off-course betting in the UK before and after the 1960 Act showed little change (Cornish 1978).

However, when legislation introduces a new form of gambling then there is a rise in the number of people who gamble, e.g. the introduction of poker-machines in New South Wales, Australia (Caldwell 1972). Whether or not these 'new' gamblers were simply people who previously gambled and who merely shifted their allegiance to poker-machines is not known. It seems parsimonious to conclude that where legislation leads to the general availability of the main forms of gambling then a greater percentage of the population will participate; most in moderation, as will be shown later, but also a small percentage at a high frequency, some of whom seek help at a crisis point caused by their gambling. The latest development in gambling legislation concerns these so-called 'compulsive gamblers'. In some states in the US laws have been enacted that establish the principle of social responsibility for compulsive gamblers and sets aside funds for the provision of help.

Participation in gambling

In any country where at least some forms of gambling are legalised and generally available a variety of opinion polls supports the conclusion that 80–90 per cent of the adult population participate. However, for two-thirds of these 'gamblers' involvement will be restricted to infrequent lotto or raffle participation and/or bets, often in the form of a sweep with friends or workmates, on one or two of the major sporting events, such as the Derby, the Melbourne Cup or the World Series. Only about one-third of the adult population regularly bet each week. The form their betting takes will vary according to availability: thus in the UK it is football pools; in Europe, the United States and in Australia, lotteries. Where poker-machines are available in social settings such as bars and social clubs it is likely that they too are used about once a week by about one in three of the adult population. The ratio of men to women among these weekly betters is about 2 : 1

although a ratio of 1 : 1 for poker- machines is more likely (Caldwell 1972). At this level of participation there are no clearly established age or socio-economic status relationships.

Regular weekly off-course betting on horse or dog races involves only about 60 per cent of the adult population. At this level of betting the ratio of men to women is about 4 : 1 and the trend extends, with fewer and fewer women involved as frequency of gambling increases. High-frequency usage of poker-machines and bingo as gambling outlets are the main candidates for the greater involvement of women than men: for bingo, the ratio may be of the order of 4 : 1. Regular involvement in casino gambling is likely to account for about one in 1,000 of the adult population. At the higher levels of gambling there are no age differences other than an under-representation of the 18–21s and the over-65s, which may well be accounted for in terms of lower income. In addition, except for casino gambling, high-frequency gambling is associated with a significantly greater proportion of skilled and semi-skilled manual workers and disproportionately fewer professional and managerial workers. Most opinion polls substantiate the relationship between higher socio-economic status and casino gaming. Regular casino gambling is associated with a ratio of men to women of 3 : 1 and younger men (21–34 years) are over-represented.

Expenditure on gambling

For any moralist wishing to establish that a nation has 'gone to the dogs' they might need to look no further than a comparison of expenditure figures for a nation's defence, housing and health budgets, with total expenditure on gambling. Thus the Rothschild Report (HMSO 1978) gave the following in £ billion for the UK: gambling 7.1, defence 5.6, housing 4.7, health 6.5. However, if on average across all forms of gambling almost 90 per cent of this expenditure is returned in winnings, it can be seen that 'turnover' figures are misleading. Despite this, the remaining 10 per cent lost or spent is in 1980 terms likely to be something over a billion pounds and is the largest single component of the total leisure industry.

In terms of overall weekly family or household expenditure on gambling, the figures derived from opinion polls are by today's values of the order of £1 (stakes less winnings). The comparisons drawn with expenditure on alcoholic drinks, tobacco or entertainments suggest that net expenditure on gambling accounts for about one-tenth of the total expenditure on all such pleasure/leisure activities. However, as two-thirds of the population bet only a few times each year such weekly expenditure figures are of doubtful value. Certainly the distribution of gambling expenditure must be highly skewed, with a small percentage of the population accounting for a disproportionately large amount of the total expenditure. Thus in the UK it has been estimated that 1.5 per cent of the adult population accounted for more than half of the total stake on horse and dog races. It has been suggested that this very skewed distribution, together with the underestimation of expenditure by heavier gamblers, causes opinion polls to generate figures that fall well short of reality (HMSO 1978).

Despite the patchiness of the data on gambling expenditure there is reasonable evidence to support the view that for most betters, regardless of their preferred form of gambling, their participation is moderate, their expenditure is likely to be planned and winnings are spent on 'home centred' items (Downes *et al.* 1976). For the 5 per cent or so of the adult population who bet 2–3 days per week on poker-machines or off-course on horses and dog races, and the 0.1 per cent of regular casino gamblers, our knowledge of expenditure, stakes, winnings and losses remains a matter for speculation. Very little is known about such gamblers and the few data available are reviewed in Chapter 4 where it is proposed that it is simply because we know so little about high-frequency or regular gamblers that gamblers who seek help appear so deviant from the moderation of the majority of gamblers described above.

From the above descriptions it can be assumed that participation in gambling of the adult population of countries where there is reasonable availability of at least lotteries and off-course betting, is as follows:

About 80–90% gamble a few times a year,

About 30% gamble on lotteries, football pools or poker-machines most weeks,

About 5% gamble regularly 2–3 times each week.

Of the latter group of regulars, most bet off-course on horse and dog races; 1 in 50 uses casino gaming as their main outlet; 1 in 8 may be a 'compulsive gambler'.

Chapter 3

Explanations of why people gamble

The concern in this chapter is to consider the general question of the motives underlying engagement in gambling. As we have seen in Chapter 2, most people, to a greater or lesser extent, use some form of gambling. Why do 80 per cent or more of the population participate in gambling? The review below examines a range of answers to this question; they come from sociology, decision theory and the psychology of individual differences. The theoretical explanations of the persistence at gambling under conditions of financial loss exhibited by compulsive gamblers are considered separately, in Chapter 5.

Sociological perspectives

Thomas (1901) considered the ability to manage unpredictable events to be an instinctive one, of evolutionary importance. The absence of much uncertainty in organised society, particularly at work, resulted in this instinctive drive finding satisfaction in gambling; i.e. people gamble because it's in their very nature. As Oldman (1978) wryly noted, such a theoretical position turns the question of, why people gamble upon its head – it becomes, why do people work? However, most general theories of gambling assume some form of human dissatisfaction or deprivation (Caldwell 1972, Downes *et al.* 1976, Cornish 1978).

Caillois (1962) hypothesised that societies can be described in terms of certain broad principles, derived from the sociology of play, which characterise their operation. The two principles that are of concern here were called *agon* and *alea*, the former applying to competitive games and the latter to those governed totally by chance or fate. Western societies founded on rationality and meritocracy were typical of games governed by *agon*. In such societies, it was argued, games of chance (*alea*) tended to abolish natural or acquired individual differences. Such games provided an outlet when hard work and personal skills were powerless to achieve success.

Devereux (1968) considered gambling to be an institutionalised pattern of deviance that developed out of the magical and religious practices of man endeavouring to cope with the problems of uncertainty and fate. For Devereux the Protestant work ethic of diligence and thrift was inherently frustrating within a capitalist system. Gambling was defined as an instrumental activity 'directed towards a consciously recognised economic end' and an 'expressive activity enjoyed as an end in itself' (Devereux 1968: 53–4). Thus, in answer to the question of why people gamble, one of the most influential sociological theorists proposed two themes of motivation, one arising from a dissatisfaction with economic status and the other associated with the satisfying subjective experience of the gambling activity itself.

Zola's (1964) descriptions of the gambling of customers in a New England bar and grill have been interpreted as providing support for both of these aspects of motivation. The gamblers here hit out at 'the system' by exercising some control over their fate, and within their group of fellow drinkers and gamblers they enjoyed personal recognition for their successes. In a similar way Yorkshire coal-miners in the town of Ashton (UK) were observed to gamble heavily (Dennis, Henriques & Slaughter 1969); gambling pervaded and dominated their leisure activities. The authors proposed that the miners' motives for gambling were based on the knowledge that escape from the limitations of their life, the insecurity of the heavy, dirty, dangerous work, could come not from saving money but only from a really big win.

Other studies have lent support to the economic motive. In her study of pools gamblers in Sweden, Tec (1964) showed that, compared with non-gamblers, they were more concerned to improve their job prospects and were more dissatisfied with their level of income. Winning on the pools was seen as a possible road to improving their standard of living. This was also supported by the UK study by Downes *et al*, (1976) who concluded that those people who were potentially upwardly mobile did the pools.

Goffman (1969), in a well-known essay entitled 'Where the action is', emphasised the manner in which the activity of gambling itself satisfied subjective emotional needs. 'Action' was defined in terms of activities that are perceived as consequential and problematic but nonetheless avoidable. Such activities are not normally available at work or at home but are associated with competitive sport, non-spectator risky sports, pool halls, bowling alleys, amusement centres, racetracks and casinos. The concept of 'action' involves far more than gambling as the following quotation makes clear:

> Looking for where the action is, one arrives at a romantic division of the world. On one side are the safe and silent places, the home, the well-regulated roles in business, industry and the professions; on the other are all those activities that generate expression, requiring the individual to lay himself on the line and place himself in jeopardy during a passing moment. (Goffman 1969: 204–5)

A person chooses to gamble as but one way of being 'in the action'. The casino was the focal point of Goffman's observations but the subjective excitement of engaging in gambling has been observed in a variety of betting environments. In the betting offices in the East End of

London, Newman (1972) described customer reactions to the race commentary ranging from indifference through concentrated listening to wild excitement. In addition to excitement the social and skill aspects of gambling have been thought to be motivational components of gambling. (Newman 1972). Thus gamblers, it was proposed, develop a specialised knowledge, enjoy consultations with other gamblers, and form judgements and take decisions not available in the normal routines of living. These themes draw a little support from studies where social interaction amongst gamblers has been observed and when bet selection has been seen to be cautious, thoughtful and controlled (Zola 1964; Herman 1967; Newman 1972).

Other sources are contradictory. Downes *et al.* (1976) found that most people don't discuss the pools and most people use chance systems for completing their forecasts (Smith & Razzell 1975). In both off-course betting and casinos, gambling tends to be associated with little time or opportunity to talk and socialise (Dickerson 1974; Downes *et al.* 1976; Oldman 1978). These data are not necessarily in conflict provided no attempt is made to generalise to all forms of gambling. Thus completing the pools and joining in lotteries are subjective private affairs not necessarily associated with cognitive skills or social interaction. On the other hand, betting on horse and dog races either at the track (Herman 1967), or in a bar (Zola 1964), may be both sociable and skilful. However, in purpose-built gambling environments where continuous betting is possible then communication with other gamblers is minimal and the skill component may be irrelevant, as in roulette, or undermined by the excitement or action.

This illustrates one of the major weaknesses of general theories of gambling and the problems inherent in the initial broad question of why people gamble. It is already apparent that unless the circular argument of Thomas (1901) is accepted a different set of answers must be sought for different forms of gambling, although some aspects of general theories have been supported by research evidence – the study by Downes *et al*. (1976) failed to reject any sociological theory. The very flexibility of such theories is perhaps a weakness.

Cornish's (1978) able review of this area emphasised the practical considerations associated with the decision to select one particular form of gambling as opposed to any other. In gaming, the fees, the pay-out ratios, the speed of play, may all be less attractive to the poorer gambler who may prefer the higher pay-offs, or regular small wins for small stakes to be found in pools, lotteries, bingo and betting on horse and dog races. Similarly a person's way of life may be more or less compatible with certain forms of gambling rather than others, or with no gambling at all. If a person is engaged in political or community activities he is less likely to gamble (Downes *et al*. 1976), possibly because he simply has less spare time available. Environmental practicalities such as the availability of gambling, e.g. the greater number of betting offices in areas where there are disproportionate numbers of lower socio-economic groups, the provision of free buses to casinos, the positioning of easily understood games nearest the casino entrance, are all determinants of the decision to gamble.

The following explanatory model was proposed by Cornish (1978). He assumed that there was an initial sense of dissatisfaction (reduced or enhanced by individual differences) which generated a readiness to seek out and experience compensatory activities, one of which might be gambling. The initial selection of a particular form of gambling would depend upon the information and facilities available and, although associated with some of the social class factors noted above, would essentially be fortuitous. Cornish proposed that, once participating in a particular form of gambling, the very process of gambling transformed the initial general dissatisfaction into particular motives, whether excitement, skill or entertainment, and then satisfied them. Hence a person learns to be satisfied by his chosen form of gambling. This model has good face validity and the extent to which it needs modification will be re-examined in the light of findings in other areas of research.

Decision theory: probabilities, pay-offs and illusions

Many laboratory studies have been completed by behavioural scientists employing mainly undergraduate subjects playing what appear to be gambling games or intellectual 'teasers' such as the 'prisoner's dilemma'. The purpose of these studies has been to understand, control, and predict how subjects will behave in laboratory situations where the games include a desirable goal and a lack of certainty that it can be attained.

The assumption is that of rationality, with decisions being made with a view to achieving some preferred state of the universe, albeit one described upon a piece of card. Edwards (1955) described four mathematical models that were developed to understand such decision-making:

1 EV – expected value: predicts that choices will be a simple function of objective probabilities and values.
2 SEV – subjective expected value: choices will be a function of individual subjective probability estimates and objective values.
3 EU – expected utility: choices will be a function of objective probabilities and subjective estimates of the worth of a goal or outcome.
4 SEU – subjective expected utility: in this model both probabilities and outcome values are subjectively estimated.

Most of the research has focused on the first and last models, EV and SEU. The simple EV model has not received strong support in laboratory settings but Cornish (1978) suggested that it may well have predictive power for human behaviour in real-life settings where the individual has good objective information concerning probabilities and values and where his or her goal is to make a relatively stable income. Under such conditions rational economic considerations may predominate.

In real-life gambling settings EV has not convincingly accounted for betting behaviour but more recent research carried out in casino settings has provided support for the EV model (e.g. Goodman *et al.* 1979). In some senses it could be said that any gambling is irrational as EV is less than zero – average pay-back ranges from 30–90 per cent depending on the form of gambling. Although there is some evidence that most on-course horse-race gambling is partly determined by rational economic considerations, long-odds, high pay-off horses may be overvalued and vice versa (McGlothin 1954).

The SEU model has fared rather better in laboratory studies, with a 50–70 per cent success rate in predicting choices between two outcomes (Kogan & Wallach 1967). These same authors, however, proposed that gambling choices in the laboratory might be better understood in terms of a subjective preference for a certain level of risk – this will be discussed in more detail in the next section, covering individual differences. In the laboratory, seeking risk might well be associated with the artificial nature and sometimes boring aspects of the methods used. The failure of the field of experimental gaming to relate to the real world has been noted (Pruitt & Kimmel 1977) and both the boredom of the tasks and, more important, the absence of any opportunity for subjects to lose money undermines most laboratory findings.

Observations in real gambling environments suggest that gamblers alter their bet preferences within a sequence of gambles, e.g. at the race track they shun favourites in the last race and raise their stakes more after a losing sequence than after winning. In an observational study in a casino in Salzburg, Hochauer (1970) found roulette players (she covertly watched 16 gamblers place between 3 and 1,077 bets) showed a preference for long shots, avoiding the 'almost fair' bets. However, Oldman (1978) observed that regular roulette players – those who played most nights of the week – used strategies of staking money at odds of around 4 : 1. It is clear that if gambling in real-life settings is to be better understood we need detailed observations and insight into gamblers' thinking as they carry out a sequence of gambles. At present we know little or nothing about bet selection processes and how they may vary, from one individual to another and from the beginner to the regular punter.

When reviewing the decision-making aspects of gambling two important phenomena illustrating the irrationality of gamblers' thinking and deciding need to be considered – the gambler's fallacy (sometimes referred to as the Monte Carlo fallacy) and the illusion of control. The former is often associated with the work of Cohen (1972) and refers to the gambler's over-estimation of likely success on a bet, following a sequence of incorrect predictions or losing bets: conversely the gambler is less sure of success following a winning bet. This fallacy holds even where outcomes are totally unrelated events, as in roulette or horse-races. Such evidence as exists for gamblers in real-life settings provides support for this fallacy and 'chasing' (see Ch. 4) may be an extreme example of it.

The illusion of control (Langer 1975) is another illustration of the fact that people fail to behave in ways that are compatible with their knowledge of the laws of chance. Ellen Langer defined this illusion as 'an expectancy of a personal success probability inappropriately higher than the objective probability would warrant'. (Langer 1975: 313). In common language, the illusion of control has been used to refer to situations in which people treat chance events as if they were under their control, or perceive games of chance as games of skill. In a series of six experiments Langer explored various aspects of this phenomenon. Her work illustrates various essential features of research methodology that have not generally been found in experimental studies on gambling. To illustrate this, one of her experiments will be considered in some detail.

Lottery tickets sold in real-life settings were used in three of the six experiments. In the second, men and women office-workers in two firms were the subjects. In each case one employee ran the lottery, on the tickets of which appeared famous football players, and the draw for a $50 prize was timed to coincide with the 1973 USA Superbowl game. As various sports pools and draws were common in both offices there was no need to provide any elaborate explanation or justification for the lottery. From the illusion of control the prediction was made that people who chose their lottery ticket would be more optimistic about winning than people who were simply handed their ticket. Thus subjects paid their dollar and selected a ticket, or were handed a ticket. On the morning of the draw the ticket seller approached each person individually and said 'Someone in the other office wants to get into the lottery but since I'm not selling tickets any more he asked me if I'd find out how much you'd sell your ticket for. It makes no difference to me but how much should I tell him?'

For those who had chosen their tickets the average selling price was $8.67 whereas those people who had had no opportunity to choose were prepared on average to sell for a price of $1.96. Thus people who chose their ticket in a game of chance were presumably more optimistic about winning and sought a significantly higher price when asked to sell. The remaining studies demonstrated that for other chance-determined gambling games the illusion of control appeared under conditions of competitiveness, familiarity with the game and when there was a greater degree of personal involvement in the game.

Although this illusion was then demonstrated in a laboratory setting (Langer & Roth 1975) it has not been replicated. In a recent series of carefully designed studies (Ladouceur & Mayraud 1981) the results failed to confirm predictions derived from the illusion of control. However, the task or gamble was to make predictions concerning coin-tossing outcomes, the subjects were university students, and no money exchanged hands. The artificial nature of such a task is remote from the reality of, for example, the casino roulette player placing 1,077 consecutive bets (Hochauer 1971). Langer herself openly admitted that in addition to her six successful studies there were two preliminary failures to achieve the predicted illusion of control effect; both studies involved subjects imagining what they would do if certain gambling events occurred. She concluded that once a person is actually in the situation then the greater the similarity between the chance situation and a skill situation, the greater will be the illusion of control.

In real gambling environments evidence of the illusion has been noted. Goffman (1969) reported that blackjack dealers who experienced runs of losing sequences might lose their jobs. Oldman (1978) interestingly observed the illusion of control exhibited in the casino operators' management of a roulette table that was losing; first a part-time croupier would be replaced by a regular, more experienced, person and finally the floor manager himself would take over if the table continued to lose. When confronted with the illogicality of such actions staff accepted the laws of chance that governed the game but felt they had to do something. Dice players, too, have been observed to roll softly for low numbers and throw hard for high (Henslin 1967). Conversely, in the laboratory setting, when the sequence of dice play was made unfamiliar by rolling but not seeing the result and then staking, smaller bets were placed (Strictland, Lewick: & Katz 1966).

As far as the provision of various forms of gambling is concerned, Langer's work has direct implications for encouraging gamblers to gamble more heavily. This can be achieved by encouraging the development of inappropriate beliefs concerning the probability of winning and the degree of skill involved. Hess & Diller (1969) gave examples of casino operators' attempts to create the impression that gambling was financially rewarding by announcing *keno ticket winners and poker-machine jack-

* Long-odds lottery.

pots; all to suggest that someone was regularly 'hitting it big'.

Individual differences

Recent theorising in the psychology of individual differences assumes that human behaviour is a function of an interaction between personality characteristics and the environment. There have been relatively few studies examining the personality of people who gamble. The underlying assumptions have been that some people were more at risk of becoming gamblers or had particular needs that could be fulfilled by gambling. Most of the literature examining specific personality concepts has been concerned with the explanation of why some people become compulsive gamblers (this work is summarised in the next chapter). Very few studies have focused on the majority of 'ordinary' punters; the work of Igor Kusyszyn has been the one exception. He studied the personality and risk-taking characteristics of race-track spectators whose gambling ranged from none to frequent (Kusyszyn & Kallai 1975; Kusyszyn & Rutter 1978; and in Lester 1979) and found no differences in personality measures in relation to the degree of engagement in betting. When compared with psychology students race-track gamblers were healthier, with lower hostility and family discord. The remainder of the literature is essentially speculative.

The theme encountered in the decision-theory research (Kogan & Wallach 1967), that risk *per se* may be sought after, has also been examined as a personality characteristic. The evidence in support of a risk-seeking trait has been contradictory but perhaps the most promising area for future research is to be found in the work of Zuckerman (1971, 1979) who defines risk-seeking within a general scale of sensation seeking. Factor analysis of the sensation-seeking scale (SSS) has confirmed four factors (Zuckerman, Eysenck & Eysenck 1978).

1 Thrill and adventure seeking as in dangerous and challenging sports.
2 Experience seeking – seeking out new environments and events to be experienced cognitively or through the senses.
3 Disinhibition – the need to act freely in the social sphere; drinking, parties, variety of sexual partners.
4 Boredom susceptibility – an aversion to repetitive events; restlessness when there is no variation in experience.

It is hypothesised that when we perceive risk in a particular situation, anxiety proportional to the risk is experienced. High levels of anxiety will be associated with withdrawal from, or avoidance of, the situation. However, the situation may also contain elements of novelty and new experiences that generate a sensation-seeking or 'approach' state. There is some evidence to confirm that people who score high on the SSS evaluate many situation as less risky than do low scorers. In addition, in novel situations high sensation seekers respond with less anxiety and more of what Zuckerman calls the 'surgency–elation effect', i.e. subjectively pleasurable excitement. The combination of lower anxiety and excitement may result in the person choosing to enter risky situations, and continuing to do so if the subsequent interaction is rewarding. Drug abuse has been related to sensation-seeking scores (Zuckerman 1979) but there are as yet no data on gamblers.

The concept of physiological arousal has also been linked with gambling (Berlyne 1967). Taking risks in different forms of gambling was assumed to generate rises and falls in arousal from staking to discovering the outcome of the bet. Such a process might help maintain an optimum level of arousal which was the basic premise of Berlyne's motivational theory. In fact Rule and Fischer (1970), using heart rate as a measure, found increased arousal, particularly in the moments just before a decision to bet was made, and in association with larger stakes. In a later paper the selection of riskier bets and increasing stakes after losing were associated with a precondition of high arousal rather than low arousal (Rule, Nutter & Fisher 1971) – a finding interpreted as contradicting the supposed role of gambling in generating an optimum level of arousal. However, as both studies were completed in the laboratory and used students provided with gaming chips, it is difficult to believe that they have much bearing on the real world of gambling.

Two other psychological concepts have seen service in the explanation of gambling behaviour: need for achievement (nAch.) and locus of control. The former derives from the personality theory of Murray (1938) who proposed a theory of human motivation based on primary needs, such as for water, air, food and necessary life-sustaining activities, and secondary or psychogenic needs, such as dominance, sex, play and achievement. It has been suggested that high nAch persons would prefer bets of greatest uncertainty or forms of gambling that involve an element of skill. The evidence is confusing and this may well arise from the method of measuring nAch: subjects respond to the Thematic Apperception Test pictures by telling stories about the persons depicted. The scoring of such a test is inherently unreliable and factors such as verbal intelligence are obviously involved.

Locus of control (Rotter 1975) is a concept defined in terms of the extent to which people believe that their own efforts, skills or actions, as opposed to chance or fate, control or influence what happens to them. People who are high on internal control have been found to be 'better than' externals in controlling or avoiding negative outcomes, e.g. internal tubercular patients know more about their illness, internal prisoners know more about parole, internals are more likely to quit smoking permanently, internals manage social embarrassment better than externals. The concept has broad face validity but has perhaps been extended too far beyond its original conceptualisation as an important; even integral, component of social learning theory (Lefcourt 1980). As far as gambling is concerned the obvious propositions arising from locus of control are that internals and externals may differentially select skill and chance gambles respectively and that persistence at gambling when losing will be more likely for internals, who will perceive their losses as determined by their own skill. There is no available evidence regarding the choice of form of gambling but Levitz (1971) found that subjects who persisted longer at a laboratory prediction task and lost most money were more likely to think that the results were determined more by skill than by chance factors. This is obviously very similar to the findings in relation to the illusion of control and we can add the possibility that internals may be more susceptible to the illusion, preferring to believe that their gambling behaviour is governed by skill even when the form of gambling is chance determined. Thus we might ask whether people who use systems at roulette or in lotteries, or believe that they are skilful in poker-machine play, score higher on internal locus of control. There are conflicting data from studies involving high-frequency and compulsive gamblers and we shall consider these later, in Chapter 4.

It would seem that the psychology of individual differences has contributed little toward answering our general question concerning the motivation to gamble. As the majority of people gamble it it is perhaps illogical to consider that any one factor of individual differences could explain the behaviour. Although there are some interesting theoretical concepts available, future research needs to address the relationship between personality factors and the level of engagement in different forms of gambling. To have validity such studies would need to be longitudinal and provide insight into the development of involvement in gambling activities.

Conclusions

In summarising this chapter it is helpful to reconsider the model proposed by Cornish (1978). It can be summarised as follows:

1　A subjective experience of 'dissatisfaction'.
2　A chance-determined 'choice' of one form of gambling in the context of a range of related factors such as information about gambling, availability, peer gambling behaviour, socio-economic status, personal disposable income, time availability, etc.
3　A learnt enjoyment or satisfaction from continued engagement in gambling.

In relation to 3, the continued involvement in a form of gambling, we may add the following:

(a)　From decision theory research, that the selection of bets will in part be a function of the person's subjective probability and value estimates.
(b)　From the illusion of control, that a person will stake higher and persist longer if he or she perceives the gambling as skill-determined, if it is a form of gambling that is well known to them and if they feel a sense of involvement or competition in the activity.
(c)　From the psychology of individual differences, that higher levels of engagement in gambling, i.e. high-frequency or regular gambling, may be associated with higher scores on measures of sensation-seeking and internal control.

Chapter 4

Who are they and how do they gamble?

Definitions and labels

In the literature, gamblers who bet frequently, lose heavily and come to the attention of psychologists, psychiatrists and self-help agencies such as GA have been variously labelled as:

pathological	(Skinner 1953; Bolen & Boyd 1968 Moran 1970a; Custer 1982)
compulsive	(Bergler 1957; Barker & Miller 1966a; Seager 1970; Geha 1970; Pokorny 1972; Dickerson & Weeks 1979; Politzer & Morrow 1980; Blaszczynski *et al.* 1982)
addicts	(Kusyszyn 1972; Koller 1972).

Most writers have assumed that the dominating feature of such gamblers is that they experience an overwhelming urge to bet. In addition to this notion of loss of control a pot-pourri of other characteristics have been appended. There have been few attempts to define and estimate excessive or problem gambling in non-clinical groups of gamblers (Dickerson 1974), and there have been no adequate operational definitions of 'compulsive', etc., gamblers. Most of the definitions have been associated with a particular theoretical standpoint and will be considered in some detail in the next chapter. Here we may note that the point made by Clark (1966), that epidemiological estimates of the number of alcoholics in a population were a function of the definition adopted, holds true for compulsive gamblers. Estimates of their numbers in the US and the UK have varied by factors of 6 and 10 respectively. The present informed guess used in the United States and Australia is just under 1 per cent of the adult population, giving the following estimates of compulsive gamblers;

United States   1,100,000
United Kingdom   350,000
Australia   80,000

In this chapter the objective is to piece together information from two main sources: studies reporting empirical data from gamblers who have sought treatment or help (we shall call these people compulsive gamblers); and data derived from the observation of people in real-life gambling environments. These we shall call regular, high-frequency or habitual gamblers, implying that they use their preferred form of gambling three or more times per week. This pragmatic non-theoretical definition should help in answering the question, 'Do compulsive gamblers differ from regular gamblers, and if so, in what ways?' Although this is essentially a descriptive chapter this consideration will be borne in mind throughout as the characteristics of compulsive and regular gamblers are reviewed. In the interests of clarity, as the direct observational work of Dickerson (1974, 1979) for UK off-course betters, Oldman (1974, 1978) for UK casino roulette players and Caldwell (1972) for Australian poker-machine players has been extensively quoted in the subsequent sections, only the information from other sources has been referenced.

Characteristics of compulsive and regular gamblers

Demographic characteristics

All reports of compulsive gamblers, whether from GA

surveys or treatment programmes, find an average age in the mid-thirties but with a range from twenty to seventy-one years (Blaszczynski *et al.* 1982). A comparison of regular off-course betters and compulsive gamblers (GA members who previously bet off-course on horse and dog races) found that the former were significantly younger. There is some evidence to suggest that if people are going to become high-frequency gamblers they tend to do so before the age of twenty-five. This may not be true of all forms of gambling, as the average age of poker-machine players has been found to be about forty years.

Usually, population surveys agree that as many women as men gamble at low frequencies but as frequency increases the proportion of women gamblers decreases. Thus in the UK only 2 per cent of high-frequency off-course gamblers are women. This is true for gambling in general but it is reasonable to suppose that this relationship does not hold for certain forms of gambling, such as poker machines where observation would suggest that women are at least equally represented among high-frequency players. This is supported by the different ratio of men to women in GA groups in the UK and Australia. In the former about 1–2 per cent of members are women (usually card or roulette gamblers) and in Australia between 5 and 10 per cent of members are women (nearly all of whom are poker-machine players).

There have been few attempts to assess the socio-economic status of high-frequency gamblers. Oldman (1974) in defining some of the prerequisites for regularly playing roulette noted that such gamblers would be used to handling large cash sums. This meant the 'regulars' were usually self-employed business people – bookies, dealers, retail traders, landlords and others with realisable assets. For the off-course gambler in the UK, semi-skilled and unskilled manual workers were found in proportions greater than one would predict from the population in general (Cornish 1978). Similar findings were reported for GA members and those entering treatment programmes

(Dickerson 1974). Whether these data represent a real difference in social class participation in high-frequency gambling is impossible to tell, e.g. the availability of certain types of gambling environments may be differentially associated with areas of greater density of semi-skilled and unskilled workers (Newman 1972). When off-course betting offices situated in a city centre were sampled the distribution of occupations did not significantly differ from the population in general.

Personality characteristics

Table 4.1 summarises the reports in the literature that have given the results of psychological assessments of gamblers. All except McGlothin (1954) and Malkin (1981) refer to compulsive gamblers, testing usually being completed as a part of an initial screening prior to treatment. None, except the small study by Wong (1980) and the carefully designed work of Malkin (1981), collected data on control or comparison groups; test scores of gamblers were merely compared with the normative data produced in the original standardisation of the test. Therefore there are insurmountable problems of interpretation. For example, the data from the two studies showing 'above average' external control (a belief that events in one's life are determined by factors outside one's control, by chance or fate, etc.) might appear to be in conflict with the data to be reviewed later that suggest that high-frequency (and possible compulsive gamblers) tend to perceive their betting to be governed more by skill factors than by chance. However, all the data collected by Wong (1980) and probably most of Moran's (1970c) were based on the questionnaire responses of GA members who would, at the weekly meeting, read out Step Two in the Recovery Programme: 'Came to believe that a power greater than ourselves could restore us to a normal way of thinking and living.' In the absence of any normative data for gamblers on intelligence or personality measures it is impossible to evaluate scores from groups of compulsive gamblers selected on the

Table 4.1 Personality characteristics of gamblers

Study	Gamblers	N	Characteristic	Result
Moran (1970c)	Pathological	41	Locus of Control (SRI)	More external than norms
Wong (1980)	GA Members	20	Locus of Control (SRI)	More external than norms
Moran (1970c)	Pathological	48	Extraversion and neuroticism (EPI)	High on neuroticism
Seager (1970)	Compulsive	16	Extraversion and neuroticism (EPI)	High on neuroticism
Wong (1980)	GA members	20	Extraversion and neuroticism (EPI)	High on extraversion
Blaszczynski et al. (1982)	Compulsive	20	Extraversion and neuroticism (EPI)	High on neuroticism
McGlothin (1954)	Women poker players	—	Adjustment (Bell)	'Better' emotional/social adjustment
Moravec (1980).	Compulsive	—	Intelligence (WAIS)	Above average
Wong (1980)	GA members	20	Impulsivity (Barratt)	Within normal range
Malkin (1981)	GA members and social gamblers	16	Myers–Brigg Locus of Control	No differences on any measures

basis of their attendance for treatment. Even the preliminary summary (Moravec 1980) of the personality data collected at the Veterans Administration programme for compulsive gamblers in Miami (a battery of seven psychological tests is routinely administered) appeared to have a somewhat dated concern for measuring 'internal' determinants of personality: 'It appears to me that the pathological gambler's fear and anxiety of being unaccepted and unloved is transformed into an obsessive, insatiable need for affection and reassurance of being loved and that the maladaptive gambling behaviour is driven by this obsessive insatiable need.' (Moravec 1980) It is unfortunate that a less restrictive assessment approach was not adopted; one that assessed the cognitions and feelings of gamblers in a range of specific situations might provide much more useful information.

As light relief from this rather barren area of psychological research Campbell (1976) asked a sample of the general population, 'Who wants to be a professional gambler?' He assessed attitudes using the Strong Vocational Interest Blank with the additional items, 'be a professional gambler' and 'interested in taking a chance'. The items that correlated significantly and positively with 'be a professional gambler' were:

- be an auto racer
- pursue bandits in a sheriff's posse
- play poker
- be a jet pilot
- be a professional athlete
- be a secret service agent.

These are a set of 'machismo' and masculine items and indeed the predominance of male interest in gambling was significant across all types of employment. Those who were not interested in becoming a gambler expressed an interest in working for a fixed salary, regular hours of work, music, art and sewing!

Given the present state of knowledge concerning the personality and other psychological characteristics of compulsive, or for that matter, any gamblers, it is unfortunate that two of the most influential writers in this area of research, Custer and Moran, continue to state that certain people are predisposed to becoming pathological gamblers 'by certain characteristics of make-up and personality' (Moran 1979) and by 'premorbid personality traits such as superior intelligence, vigorously competitive . . .' (Custer 1982). A recent unpublished study by Malkin (1981) highlights the frailty of such assumptions. This study matched male GA members from two chapters in Western Australia for age and socio-economic status with a group of social gamblers who bet not more than twice per week and not less than once per month (a definition that approaches our present definition of 'regular'). Malkin found no differences between his groups for locus of control (Richardson 1968) or on any of the four personality characteristics measured by the Myers-Brigg questionnaire (Myers 1962): extraversion–introversion, sensation–intuition, thinking – feeling and judging – perceptual.

In conclusion, the measurement of the personality characteristics of compulsive gamblers (i.e. those seeking treatment) in the absence of a comparison group of regular or high-frequency gamblers has lead to the unjustified assumption that people with certain personality traits are more likely to gamble excessively.

Preferred form of gambling

The first question to be considered is whether compulsive gamblers use only certain forms of gambling. The different forms of gambling have been described elsewhere in terms of their structural characteristics such as payout interval, the involvement of the better, the skill required and the payout ratios and probability of winning (Weinstein & Deitch 1974). Where the view has been held that some forms of gambling were somehow more 'dangerous' than others this danger has been associated with the frequency and rapidity of the gambling sequence. Thus, prior to the first Betting and Gaming Act in the UK (1960) it was recognised by politicians of the day that the encouragement of 'continuous' betting in off-course betting offices should be avoided (Butler 1959).

The empirical data lend some support to this notion, as the following types of gambling activity have been reported by compulsive gamblers; off-and on-course betting, poker machines, roulette, blackjack, craps (in fact all casino games), bingo, pinball machines and keno. Moran (1979) would wish to add instant lottery tickets – 'heart-stoppers' – to this list and in an earlier paper mentioned a football pools gambler who had sought treatment (Moran 1970a). On the other hand, although enormous numbers of people buy raffle tickets and regularly complete lotto and pools forms, with the single exception given above, there are no reports in the literature of a person seeking help for problems associated with these forms of gambling. Thus it seems reasonable to conclude that compulsive gamblers use only certain gambling activities, particularly those where the cycle of stake and play is repeated at least once every ten minutes or so. Certainly, informal observations in UK off-course betting offices suggests that when races occur less than once every fifteen minutes customers tend not to stay and bet in a continuous fashion. However, where there is high involvement with high stakes and high skill-levels, for example in a game of poker, a slower pace may be acceptable.

Despite the poor quality of the data available it seems reasonable to conclude that compulsive gamblers are more likely to be associated with certain types of gambling, usually those with a relatively rapid sequence of staking, playing (or listening to/watching a race) and result or payout. However, one can state with certainty that it is clear that the large proportion of high-frequency gamblers using these particular games do not seek help or consider themselves to be compulsive gamblers.

Two further questions merit consideration: do compulsive gamblers use a greater number of different types of gambling activities (outlets) than high-frequency gamblers; and, secondly, do they somehow gamble in a different way from other high-frequency gamblers?

In respect of the first question it has sometimes been assumed that the hallmark of 'true' compulsive gamblers is that they will bet on anything. This characteristic has sometimes been incorporated in definitions of compulsive gambling (e.g. Bergler 1957). However, the limited data available do not confirm this view. Table 4.2 summarises data for UK betting-office customers: regular gamblers (betting whenever possible, more than 3 times per week) and compulsive gamblers (GA members who reported using betting offices at a similar frequency). The difference between the distributions is not significant and for the purposes of this discussion it must be emphasised that 23 per cent of the compulsive gamblers used only one outlet.

Table 4.2 Percentage distribution of the self-reported number of betting outlets per person for compulsive and regular off-course gamblers

Number of betting outlets	Compulsive	Regular
1	23	43
2	49	36
3	21	11
4	6	8
5	1	2

Turning to the second question, it can be clarified by considering it in respect of one particular gambling situation, such as roulette. The question then becomes, do compulsive gamblers play roulette in a different way from high-frequency gamblers? There are no empirical studies that can be brought to bear on the matter. However, Kat (1974) reported that a compulsive gambler who was a roulette player described delaying placing his chips until the very last moment. Some roulette players attending GA confirm the use of such a style and in addition describe a variety of systems that they followed at one time or another. In the casino where he worked, Oldman noted that, for those customers who played roulette every night of the week, 'it is very common for punters to wait until the ball is underway before placing bets. The call of "no more bets" is the signal for a flurry of last-minute chips.' (Oldman 1974.) In the same paper he also noted that these high-frequency gamblers often followed an individual system that governed their choice of bets. (Whether or not compulsive gamblers hold different beliefs about such systems is discussed later.) Similar themes may be true for the use of poker machines; some compulsive gamblers report using several machines at once. Casual observation in large clubs reveals that a few high-frequency players follow similar idiosyncratic patterns.

Finally, a comparison of compulsive and high-frequency gamblers who used off-course betting offices suggested that both groups were more likely to prefer single bets placed at the very last moment before the race began. In some instances this phenomenon of late betting was so extreme that two customers preferred an office that permitted betting between 'the hare's running' and 'they're off', a period of about 3–5 seconds during which there was never any mention of price changes. Both compulsive and regular off-course betters made their final bet selection in the office, often impulsively changing their decision at the last moment, whereas the low-frequency customers often entered the office with their bet already written out.

One other characteristic is the preference of both regular and compulsive gamblers to be on their own while gambling. Whether the form is roulette or off-course betting, conversation is minimal and superficial – the pace is such that concentration has to be maintained. Sometimes GA members recall viewing friendly contact with suspicion; they were fearful lest it be known how badly they fared at times, but also a 'friend' might want to borrow money. Certainly for such gamblers social contact threatened the continuity of their betting activity.

The conclusions that can be drawn in this section are:

1 Gamblers who use certain types of gambling or betting environment, particularly those with a rapid sequence of stake and play, are more likely to seek help as compulsive gamblers.

2 Compulsive gamblers and high-frequency gamblers seem to demonstrate similar patterns of betting behaviour that differ from those of the average or infrequent gambler.

Amount of time spent gambling

Although about one-third of the adult population may spend around fifteen minutes a day on some gambling activity, the difference between this level of involvement and the time spent on gambling by compulsive and high-frequency gamblers is striking. Once again, data collected from high-frequency off-course betters while in betting offices, compared with self-reported data from GA members who previously gambled off-course, provide the main grounds for concluding that the two groups are very similar in terms of the amount of time devoted to betting. Over 80 per cent of both groups reported betting on six or more races, staying on the premises for two or more hours and repeating this pattern on as many days as possible through each week. Regular punters in a casino attend most nights of the week and play roulette for several hours each night. It is difficult to imagine that compulsive roulette players could play for significantly longer periods but there are no data to confirm this. Similarly, poker machines have been reported to have been used by a compulsive gambler for three hours at any one time (Barker & Miller 1966a). Casual observation and discussion with club managers and staff suggests that a few club members play the poker machines for an hour or longer most nights of the week. From Caldwell's (1972) figures on amounts lost in a session of poker-machine playing it can be estimated that 2 per cent of players had sessions of over one hour (i.e. those who reported losing between $30 and $40 during their last session of play).

In conclusion it appears that high-frequency gamblers and compulsive gamblers may spend between fifteen and thirty hours per week carrying out their preferred betting or gaming. Such a level may be sustained, on average, by both groups for more than ten years. When compulsive gamblers have been asked to differentiate between their early or non-problematic level of betting as opposed to their later heavy or compulsive level, estimates of the latter range from an average of four years to over ten years (Seager 1970; Wray 1980, Blaszczynski *et al*. 1982). The sheer volume of gambling carried out by high-frequency and compulsive gamblers is awesome. That it is commonly maintained for up to a decade or longer is extraordinary.

Money spent on gambling

If the frequency and amount of time spent betting is similar for both high-frequency and compulsive gamblers it remains a possibility that compulsive gamblers stake, and therefore eventually lose, significantly larger sums. The evidence for this is not impressive. Certainly the size of debts reported by compulsive gamblers at the time they seek help may range from $100 to $35,000 in Australia (Blaszczynski *et al*. 1982), and from £350 to an average high of £1,200 for GA members in Scotland (Brown 1973). In the United States the typical client attending the Compulsive Gambling Counselling Centre, Johns Hopkins University, has debts of between $15,000 and $80,000 (Politzer & Morrow 1980). There are no data for the debts of high-frequency gamblers, although there are good grounds for assuming that such gamblers do incur debts; 56 per cent of high-frequency off-course betters reported having gambling debts but the brief structured interviews did not seek information regarding the size of these debts. Oldman (1978) estimated that the regular roulette players in the casino where he worked might spend to a limit of £50 per night and that this would generate average losses of about £35 per week. However, he went on to point out that such a level of losing would be interspersed with 'winning weeks', the occasional 'bonanza' and the weeks when losses totalled £350 (about $700). Few people could withstand such losses without incurring, at least temporarily, some debts. Oldman took the view that the only difference between high-frequency gamblers and compulsive gamblers is that the latter have reached a financial crisis. In the absence of data to the contrary it seems reasonable to assume that the group we are here referring to as 'compulsive' may have larger gambling debts than high-frequency gamblers.

A contributing factor to the amount spent, and lost, is that both high-frequency and compulsive gamblers tend to use large stakes. Although this is not invariably the case, it is certainly borne but by members of GA recalling the difference between their average bet early in their gambling experience and their average bet just prior to seeking help (e.g. early average bet £1.21, later average bet £18.87; from Wray 1980). Similarly, the same author reported that the maximum stake size changed from an average £9.10 to an average maximum of £200.

This is a good opportunity to expand on the comment made earlier in Chapter 2 concerning the skewed nature of the distribution of gambling expenditure. The Rothschild Report (HMSO 1978) reported that more than half the total stake on horse races (£1,800 million in all in 1976) was generated by 1.5 per cent of the adult population. A similar conclusion can be drawn for poker-machine players. Seventy-one per cent of players reported losing less than $5 the last time they used the machines. However, a small minority (about 2%) recalled losing between $30 and $40. If we apply this kind of skewed distribution to the figures Caldwell (1972) gave for the gross per annum take from poker machines in one social club it suggests that about 2 per cent of players lose about $1,000 per annum (in 1971). This is ten times the average losses per annum for all club members, usually the only statistic available.

Table 4.3 Illustration of the per annum expenditure at different levels of frequency of betting

| | Social gamblers | | Regular gamblers | |
	A	B	C	D
Stake size	£1 ($2)	£1 ($2)	£2 ($4)	£3 ($6)
Bets/session	1	2	6	7
Sessions/week	1	2	4	5
Total p.a.	£52 ($100)	£208 ($400)	£2,500 ($5,800)	£5,500 ($11,000)
losses p.a.*	£5.2 ($10)	£20.8 ($40)	£250 ($500)	£550 ($1,100)

* Based on the Rothschild Report (HMSO 1978) assumption that 90 per cent of money staked was returned in winnings.

The logic that betting more frequently in a session, having more sessions in a week and using larger stakes will result in ever increasing expenditure is inescapable. Furthermore, even to the non-mathematician, it is evident that total annual expenditure is an accelerating function. This is illustrated in Table 4.3. Although hypothetical data on betting are fraught with assumptions, here the figures illustrate how relatively minor changes in betting behaviour at high frequencies may be associated with large changes in gross expenditure and losses, and may result in the precipitation of a financial crisis. Whether or not this occurs, the point to be emphasized is that high-frequency gambling needs to be very finely controlled.

Finally in this section, it has been suggested that compulsive gamblers usually have 'beginner's luck' and have a big win early in their gambling experience (Bolen & Boyd 1968, Custer 1982). The percentage of compulsive gamblers reporting an early large win ranges from 6 per cent to 40 per cent (Seager 1970, and Moran 1970a respectively). When high-frequency off-course betters were asked whether they had any particular memories of how their luck ran when they started betting, 72 per cent reported a large win or stated that their luck had been good.

Thus at this stage it appears that high-frequency and compulsive gamblers are similar in that they use large stakes, incur debts and some recall having 'beginner's luck' (they recall their early gambling as lucky; whether or not it *was* lucky is another matter). Compulsive gamblers may have significantly larger debts. (e.g. Blaszczynski *et al.* 1982).

Subjective experiences while gambling

Cognitions

Cognitions, the thoughts and beliefs of gamblers, have been little studied despite their obvious importance. The perception of their gambling as skilful or governed by chance was examined in off-course betters (Dickerson 1974); 60 per cent of high-frequency gamblers rated their bet selection as more than 50 per cent skill. The majority of less frequent betters rated their selection as 'all luck' or less than 25 per cent skill. (Oddly enough, the one sex difference in the study occurred at this point, with all the high-frequency women betters estimating that their bet selection was governed mainly by chance.) When these off-course gamblers were asked to rate their chances of winning with the betting slip they held in their hand, high-frequency gamblers were significantly more optimistic. Skill and optimism interacted; thus the less betters thought their selection skilful, the less likely they were to be sure of winning and vice versa. However, all possible combinations were reported; some thought their bet selection was 'all luck' and yet were absolutely sure they would win. Conversely, some thought their selection was predominantly skilful and yet were quite unsure that their present bet would win. The evidence from compulsive gamblers suggests that they too tend to take an optimistic view of their chances of winning. However, this conclusion was based on data from a retrospective questionnaire which asked GA members about their certainty of winning in general rather than their confidence regarding a specific bet. Once again it must be emphasized that some compulsive gamblers were very unsure of winning. For some high-frequency gamblers there is a combination of thoughts: (a) that their activity is skilful; (b) that they are confident of winning this time; and (c) that they perceive that they are losing money (83% of regular betters thought they lost money over a twelve-month period). Over a period of years this combination might have a profound effect on self-esteem.

As noted earlier, there is evidence that both high-frequency and compulsive gamblers place their bets as late as possible before the play sequence or the race begins. The explanations for this vary from gambler to gambler.

In off-course betting, gamblers usually think that to bet as late as possible means that they have the most up-to-date information before placing their bets. There is obviously some substance to such a view, as odds vary right up to the 'off'. However to bet late invariably cannot be sustained by a 'skill' argument as some information on form and rider may outweigh all later information and in such instances a better price can be obtained by staking ante-post or well before the 'off'. For roulette, Oldman (1978) considered that the late placement of chips by regular gamblers when the ball was already spinning in the roulette wheel was a reflection of their thoughts about the spinner – he worked for the club and could 'influence' which numbers came up. The only other insight into roulette players late placement came from the report of a compulsive gambler who thought that he got a greater thrill or 'buzz' by placing his chips as late as possible (Kat 1974).

The use of systems has been widely reported for most kinds of gambling (Eadington 1976) although as Oldman (1974) knowingly expressed it for roulette: 'It is true that there are many books on roulette systems with seductive titles such as *How to Win at Roulette* and much of what they say makes sound sense, except for their titles. Most "systems" are systems that slow down the speed at which the punter steadily loses his money.' Regular players usually achieve this by adopting a level of odds of about 4 : 1. However, where the game involves a skill component as, for example, in blackjack, a counting system can help the skilful player (Thorp 1966, and the Revere Advanced Point Count in Uston & Rapoport 1977). Other aspects of the decision processes of high-frequency gamblers have not been studied. It is common in GA meetings to hear members describe themselves as 'bad' gamblers; they would make the right selection before going betting but by the time the particular race came up they were already losing heavily and switched to a longer odds horse or dog at the last minute in an attempt to recoup losses. Wray's (1980) retrospective survey suggested that for GA members the change to the more frequent, problematic level of gambling was associated with more frequent last-minute changes in bet selection.

The phenomena of 'chasing', of betting more frequently with increased stakes after a sequence of losing bets, is discussed separately in the next section in the context of 'loss of control'. There is, however, a cognitive aspect of this, suggested by Lesieur (1979), which can be seen as an extension of the gambler's fallacy. Lesieur argued that for the compulsive gambler chasing was seen as logical, the right thing to do when losing, and sometimes the only possible way to retrieve a hopeless situation. Such thoughts would be sustained by seeing other gamblers periodically get out of a crisis by acting on the belief 'I'll get even tomorrow,' even if that meant gambling with borrowed or stolen money. This is an interesting and possibly important hypothesis regarding the cognitive processes of compulsive gamblers but at present it is not supported by empirical data. I have, however, heard such thoughts expressed by a young GA member as he contemplated using his favourite poker-machine: 'It owes me some.' In a similar vein, about 15 per cent of poker-machine players, men and women, say they play 'to win jackpots' rather than for amusement.

In a crisis, or when gambling has reached a problematic level, compulsive gamblers report thinking of nothing else; they become totally preoccupied with thoughts of the next opportunity to bet, how to get money, etc., and all other aspects of living are seen as an intrusion. Kusyszyn (1972) suggested that the images held by the compulsive gambler were grandiose – all too often in reality, it would seem, imagined winnings are simply to replace the losses. In fact little information is available concerning the phantasies and images entertained by regular gamblers.

Affect

Several observers have commented on the range of behaviours shown by gamblers while betting which suggest that for some the experience is exceedingly exciting or arousing (Moran 1970a; Newman 1972; Dickerson 1974; Oldman 1974; Custer 1982). Responses observed include tension, pallor, sweating, pacing up and down, shouting and swearing. Blaszczynski (1982) noted strong indications of autonomic arousal in compulsive poker-machine players. In spite of these observations only one study, a survey by Wray (1980), has systematically collected subjective reports from compulsive gamblers. He concluded that the problem level of gambling (just prior to the gambler attending GA) was typified by 'very, or extreme excitement' during a race (reported by 70%) and that there was a significant tendency for larger stakes to be employed in order to maintain the experience of excitement. However, once again, heterogeneity was the order of the day with 15 per cent rating their subjective experience as 'calm, or a little excited', and, for over a third, a bet of 10p (20 cents) was all that was required for excitement to be felt. Subjective feelings on winning also ranged from the 10 per cent who felt 'nothing much at all' to the 78 per cent who felt 'elated or happy'. Anecdotal observations at GA meetings support this heterogeneity of feelings. On winning, some gamblers reported worrying about where to hide the cash (usually from their spouse), others on losing described feeling calm and 'slept like a log', while others described vomiting after a sequence of losing bets. Some poker-machine players agreed together at one meeting that an early win while playing the machines was 'unlucky' or felt 'bad'.

It is clear, even from the fragments in the literature to date, that the subjective experience of gamblers, their cognitions and their feelings while they gamble, is an intriguing and important focus for future research. The conclusion for this section in respect of the search for differences between compulsive and high-frequency gamblers must remain at present inconclusive.

Loss of control

Some definition of 'loss of control' is usually taken to be the crucial difference between compulsive gamblers and all other gamblers. Certainly most gamblers seeking help express the view that they feel they just cannot stop gambling, that they have an overwhelming urge to gamble (Bolen & Boyd 1968; Seager 1970). One aspect of losing control is 'chasing', when the gambler reports the subjective experience of an increased urge to bet following a losing sequence; behaviour may then parallel this with continued betting, sometimes with increased stakes and/or shifts to long odds.

Ninety-six per cent of GA compulsive gamblers, previously off-course betters, reported 'chasing'; an almost identical figure (95%) was found for high-frequency off-course betters. In the same study an attempt was made to explore 'loss of control' as a dimension ranging from chasing, spending more than planned, to spending all cash in hand. Table 4.4 illustrates that the crudely defined dimension may have some face validity, with increasingly regular loss of control shown by high-frequency and compulsive gamblers. The indications are that once again compulsive gamblers may be a slightly more extreme group, reporting more frequent loss of control than comparable high-frequency off-course betters. The range of loss-of-control behaviour is also notable, with 4 per cent of compulsive gamblers reporting not chasing and one in five low-frequency or 'ordinary' betters reporting the experience of chasing. Information from poker-machine players indicated that about a quarter of both men and women players reported 'losing more than they intended' on the last occasion that they played. The size of these unplanned losses was not established but once again it indicates that engagement in gambling may be difficult for some people

Table 4.4 Aspects of loss of control for off-course betting: low-frequency, high-frequency and compulsive gamblers

	Chasing (%)	Spending more than planned		Spending all cash	
		Sometimes (%)	Regularly (%)	Sometimes (%)	Regularly (%)
Low-frequency	20	24	0	1	0
High-frequency	95	23	75	51	45
Compulsive	96	33	65	23	75

to control. Anecdotal reports by compulsive gamblers suggest that their experiences of loss of control may vary from
day to day. 'Loss of control' is also recognised by professional gamblers as an occupational hazard against which
various precautions can be taken.

Regaining control or stopping gambling

Compulsive gamblers who attend GA as a means of dealing with their problem generally stop betting immediately
(92%). About 50 per cent reported that they found it
'hard' to 'very hard' to give up gambling, about 20 per
cent that stopping was 'easy'. If the accuracy of the self-
report data is to be accepted then 60 per cent never bet
again while attending GA. However, about 30 per cent of
members report between one and eight 'falls' or 'busts'
(having a bet); 10 per cent report nine or more busts, over
a period of about three years. Another indication of the
difficulties some compulsive gamblers experience when
trying to stop is that 72 per cent report using some form
of stimulus management. That is, they report avoiding
reading the racing page or watching races, walking past
off-course betting offices, etc. (Wray 1980).

   The desire to stop gambling might be assumed to be an
obvious difference between high-frequency and compulsive gamblers but the evidence, limited though it is,
contradicts such an assumption. Of regular off-course
gamblers asked 'Do you want to stop or cut back on your
betting?', 64 per cent said 'no', 32 per cent 'would like to
cut back' and 4 per cent 'would like to stop'. Similarly,
'Have you ever tried stopping?' was answered 'never tried'
by 62 per cent, 'tried, found easy' by 6 per cent and 'tried,
found hard' by 22 per cent.

   These data were for off-course betters. There are no
studies that detail the experience of stopping or regaining
control for other types of gambling. From his descriptions
of the characteristics of recuperative compulsive gamblers
(based upon 150 GA members) Custer (1982) defined

three stages of recovery as follows:

1 Critical phase: includes honest desire for help, stops gambling, thinking clearer, spiritual needs examined, returns to work, problems being faced.
2 Rebuilding phase: paying bills, restitution plans, self-respect returning, improved relationships, developing goals, resolving legal problems, less irritating behaviour, more relaxed, less impatient.
3 Growth phase: insight into self, giving affection to others, sacrificing for others, preoccupation with gambling decreasing, problems faced promptly.

The theme is idealistic, reflects the language of GA and is similar to early psychiatric descriptions of recovery from alcoholism. None the less, many GA members who have successfully stopped gambling would see similarities between these phases of recovery and their own experiences. However, Custer's summary of 'recovery' requires verification and further research.

Cummings, Gordon and Marlatt (1980) provided some insight into the precipitants of relapses or busts. With an admittedly small sample of GA members (N = 19), they found that about half of all relapses were associated with what they called 'negative emotional states', i.e. frustration, anger and depression. Urges to gamble, testing out personal control by going into a gambling environment, and interpersonal conflicts accounted for the remaining relapses in roughly equal proportions.

Custer (1982) reported that if gamblers had just stopped betting prior to admission to hospital it was not uncommon for staff to observe 'tremulousness, headache, abdominal pain, diarrhoea, cold sweats and nightmares to occur for a few days after admission'. He suggested that these may represent withdrawal symptoms or might be due to sleep starvation. The former possibility was supported by the retrospective survey data for GA members reported by Wray and Dickerson (1981) summarised in Table 4.5. The content and frequency of these disturbances, associated with sudden cessation of gambling, were

Table 4.5   Disturbances reported by more than 20 per cent of GA
members when ceasing to gamble

Disturbance	%
Felt irritable	46
Felt restless	46
Felt depressed	39
Could not concentrate	36
Kept thinking the same thoughts over and over again	36
Felt guilty	36
Felt anxious	31
Felt jumpy	29
Felt angry	27
Felt bored	27

similar to those reported by excessive alcohol drinkers on
cessation of drinking and in such a context would be
labelled 'withdrawal' symptoms.

Once again it must be concluded that the evidence
reviewed in this section has not sustained the hypothesis
that compulsive gamblers are different from high-
frequency gamblers. Some of the latter group claim to
want to stop or control their gambling, and when they try
to do so, find it difficult. This is similar to the experience
of GA members trying to stop gambling. However, not all
such compulsive gamblers find it hard; about 20 per cent
say it was easy to stop.

Professional gamblers : similarities and differences

Within the frame of reference of this chapter it seems
appropriate to include information concerning a group of
undoubted high-frequency gamblers, namely professional
gamblers. There is no doubt such gamblers exist. The
forms of gambling upon which they focus are those that
involve skill – horseracing and card games such as blackjack and poker. To make an income consistently from
gambling requires a high frequency of betting and a high
turnover of money staked; for example a 'good' pro-

fesional gambler betting on horseracing might reckon on a 4 per cent 'profit' on total money staked.

Kusyszyn (1972) summarised what he considered to be the main characteristics of professional gamblers. He based his account on the life stories of two famous gamblers: Nick the Greek (Rice 1969) and Pittsburgh Phil (Cole 1908). The cognitive characteristics were an excellent or photographic memory, ability to concentrate for long periods of time and an ability to make accurate probability estimates. Mood or feelings during gambling should not be altered or upset by a series of losses or wins. Overall, both Nick and Phil maintained a disciplined and rational approach to gambling and kept detailed records of all bets, losses and winnings. From the exciting story of Ken Uston's role as *The Big Player* (Uston & Rapoport 1977) in a blackjack counting team, similar themes can be extracted. The time and effort involved in learning to use at speed the Revere Advanced Point Count, the planning, the teamwork, the financial investment and the record-keeping, all fit well with Kusyszyn's list of characteristics.

During this author's survey of off-course betting office customers, four men were interviewed who claimed to earn extra income by their gambling. Whether or not they were professional gamblers is open to debate but the methods of gambling described by the most convincing of the four provide data supporting the themes already outlined in this section. The man in question was about twenty-five years old and smartly suited. He did not place a bet during his visit but claimed he had an ante-post bet on a horse he named (it won in a photo-finish during the interview). He bet only during the flat-racing season, used the 'blackbook' of form each week, and had occasional tips from a friend in a stable. He said he never stayed to bet in betting offices. He carefully planned all his bets. If, for example, he was prepared to spend £20 (about $40) on four bets at a race meeting – he claimed never to bet on all races – he would divide up this total according to his own estimate of their rank order of probability of winning.

If he won or lost, it made no difference to his plans. He kept records of all bets and their outcome and claimed to have won £400 (about $800) in the last flat-racing season (1973). In terms of the survey such a person was one in four hundred customers.

It seems reasonable to conclude that a professional approach to gambling is but rarely found. Apart from the skills and hard work involved there is an explicit recognition that certain measures must be adopted to maintain self-control of gambling, such as record keeping, prior selection of bets, avoiding continuous betting and so on. Professional gamblers may experience the same pressures to lose control as any other high-frequency gambler but recognise it as a problem to be overcome.

Problems associated with compulsive gambling

Interpersonal relationships

Considering some of the basic characteristics of compulsive gambling it is not surprising that personal relationships suffer, due to the 15–30 hours spent gambling each week, the preference to gamble alone, the total pre-occupation with gambling and its related debts, etc. If one adds to this the frequent observation that gamblers are great liars – usefully documented by Wray (1980) for GA members (see Table 4.6) – then it is easy to understand why up to 50 per cent of compulsive gamblers have marital

Table 4.6   GA members' reports of lying at different stages in their gambling careers

	Early in betting career (%)	Later, at problem level (%)
Lying to cover up gambling activity, often	35	94
Lying, even when unnecessary, often	29	84

problems meriting treatment at the time they seek help. The impact of their lying is usually described in terms of the lack of confidence and trust of all those involved with the gambler, including spouse, family and employer. Apart from the prescription of marital therapy in some treatment programmes, in GA itself it is common to hear gamblers advised on ways of building up trust and also on how to accept misplaced mistrust when an anxious partner inaccurately accuses them of returning to gambling.

Financial, employment and legal problems

Usually, but not invariably, gamblers seek help when they have large debts that cannot be met. Sometimes there may be the added crisis of loss of employment together with threatened or actual legal proceedings if cash has been stolen. Malkin (1981), for example, found that half his small group of compulsive gamblers admitted to crimes of misappropriation of cash in order to meet debts and continue gambling. However, it is important to note that the ability of a gambler, (and of his surrounding family and friends) to get out of trouble will vary enormously from individual to individual. In addition some employers may accept certain levels of misappropriation in an employee of value to them. There are no detailed reports available on these matters but, as discussed earlier, debts can range up to many thousands of dollars.

In general it is estimated that the gambler entering a treatment programme has had an an adverse effect on some ten other significant people in his life (Politzer & Morrow 1980). This kind of guess may not be an exaggeration, but the whole area of the social costs of gambling has been little studied. The following details of an individual gambler's circumstances provide some insight into the costs involved.

John (41 years) illustrates the kind of costs involved. Having gambled for about eighteen years he sought help at a crisis point associated with debts of £3,000 ($6,000).

He was a skilled fitter working for a central-heating company. He also earned money from 'foreigners' (jobs completed on an *ad hoc* basis for friends and neighbours for which money would be advanced by the customer for the purchase of materials). These were his undoing as he gambled and lost such advances. When he first attended GA four of these jobs were outstanding, his wife had had no allowance for five weeks, all his wages had been lost gambling and he had a loan from a finance company on which he was failing to maintain the repayments. He had attempted suicide because he had promised his wife on two previous occasions that he would stop gambling. She worked as a part-time office-cleaner and all her earnings went to feed and clothe the family; there were four daughters. The family had not been away on holiday for five years. John was regularly absent or silent, brooding and easily irritated. The children had no interaction with him and no shared activities. John's wife was physically run down, depressed and constantly worried about the family's security and future. The customers of the four outstanding jobs were becoming abusive and one had instructed a solicitor to act to obtain repayment. John himself had become isolated from two long-standing friends as he owed them small sums of money and was now threatened with dismissal from his job as his work and attendance record had deteriorated over the last six months.

As one might reasonably expect, only those gamblers entering treatment have provided information concerning the above problems; a tiny sample ($N = 7$) of off-course gamblers was interviewed in depth by the author and despite the indication that most had some interpersonal, financial and related problems the degree of disruption seemed much less severe than for comparable GA members.

The costs to society arising from compulsive gamblers are said to be enormous (Taber 1979) but have only recently been assessed in a rigorous manner (Politzer, Morrow & Leavey 1981). Adopting practices accepted in the estimation of the indirect costs of alcoholism, the authors sampled data from clients who satisfied the DSM-III (American Psychiatric Association 1980) diagnostic criteria for 'pathological gambling' on entering the counselling programme at the Johns Hopkins University. These data were used to estimate the costs arising in four areas:

1   Lost production.
2   Costs of enforcing, adjudicating and detaining in relation to the 'average' white-collar offence committed by compulsive gamblers.
3   Costs of maintaining the gambler in prison.
4   'Abused dollars' – an estimate of the amounts obtained legally or illegally, and then gambled, which otherwise would have been used for some essential purpose.

(Categories 1–3 are accepted as measures of the indirect costs of alcoholism.)

On the basis of their data, together with the estimated 1.1 million compulsive gamblers in the US, the authors calculated the total illness costs of pathological gambling to be over thirty billion dollars per annum, placing the 'illness' among the top six in terms of societal costs. Omission of the fourth category of costs, 'abused dollars', would reduce this total by a little over a half but would still generate costs for the UK and Australia of over two billion pounds and one billion dollars per annum respectively. Whether such generalisations are justifiable is open to debate but none the less such guesses should provide a spur to further research to validate this important study.

Alcoholism and suicide

It has sometimes been supposed that compulsive gamblers may also drink to excess and have a high suicide rate. At present there are no data to suggest that the drinking habits of gamblers are any different from the rest of the population. Suicide has been noted to occur more frequently in compulsive gamblers than in the general population but no more frequently than in other comparable groups seeking help from psychiatrists (Moran 1970c).

Conclusions

It seems justifiable to conclude that similarities rather than differences between high-frequency and compulsive gamblers are the order of the day. Despite the limitations of the data it appears that both types exhibit very similar patterns of gambling behaviour but that those gamblers who seek help tend to use larger stakes and may have greater debts. In addition these compulsive gamblers may have more severe marital, employment and legal problems but but here the comparison data for regular gamblers are simply not available.

The similarities in gambling behaviour provide some resolution of the problem of definition. The decision to seek help and make contact with a helping agent does not provide a sound criterion for differentiation or for a typology. Seeking help can be precipitated by a spouse discovering a debt, by the advertisement of a treatment programme or GA meeting. Furthermore, individual thresholds for the tolerance of financial and other problems will vary enormously. The term 'compulsive' none the less may retain a common usage. 'Compulsive gambler' seems to have few of the pejorative connotations of some mental illness labels and may serve a useful role in communication among both those giving and those receiving help.

Without splitting hairs, however, 'compulsive gambling' does become a concept of questionable meaning and value. It has been established that the evidence so far accumulated in no way suggests that those who seek help gamble in a qualitatively different way from other high-frequency gamblers. What is apparent is that all such gamblers show various betting behaviours, cognitions, beliefs and affective states during gambling that are qualitatively different from average or low-frequency gamblers. If there is any evidence of two types of high-frequency gambling it is to be found in the case studies and biographies of professional gamblers. It appears that professional gambling is typified by a rational and controlled approach sustained by hours of information collection, detailed accounting and the like. Even with the limited information on professional gamblers (they are clearly very rare perhaps 1 in 1,000 of high-frequency gamblers), the characteristics of their approach to gambling support the hypothesis that all high-frequency gambling is associated with the phenomenon of subjective difficulties in maintaining self-control of the amount and frequency of betting. Rather than defining different types of gambling it may be more compatible with the evidence, and more theoretically useful, to consider self-control as an important dimension of gambling. The degree of loss of control is positively correlated with frequency – the greater the frequency the greater the pressure to lose control. High-frequency gamblers may occupy different points on such a dimension, with extreme control shown by the very few who make a living from gambling, and those with little or no control (who will be more likely to enter a crisis and seek help) at the other end of the dimension. The intermediate points may be occupied by the little-studied majority of regular gamblers who use a variety of methods of control which may vary in their efficacy from time to time during years of gambling.

Chapter 5

Why do they persist when losing?

Explanations of compulsive gambling began appearing in the scientific journals at the beginning of this century. However, even by the 1950s it would have been difficult to separate the different theoretical approaches to the problem; for example, psychiatric and psychoanalytic themes were often intertwined and psychology as the science of behaviour had contributed little except Skinner's (1953) comments drawing parallels between 'pathological' gambling and animals responding to intermittent reinforcement. Today, however, it begins to make sense to consider at least four main sources of theoretical explanations of the behaviour of compulsive gamblers: psychoanalysis, psychiatry, sociology and psychology. These will be considered in turn and the various concepts evaluated in the light of the empirical data summarised in the previous chapter.

Psychoanalytic explanations

Von Hattingberg (1914) proposed that the fear and tension inherent in gambling were sexual in nature, reflecting masochistic tendencies arising from childhood guilt in anal gratification. Dostoevsky's gambling binges were the focus of some short explanatory statements by Freud (1928); the behaviour was explained in terms of a compulsive neurotic

state with origins in the childhood compulsion to mastur-
bate. Persistence even when losing was seen as a masochistic exercise that 'balanced' the guilt generated by the
unconscious desires to eliminate a cruel father.

This proposal that compulsive gambling has its origins
in the Oedipal desire for the mother's love and the father's
decease has not been seriously challenged in the psychoanalytic literature. It was extensively used by Bergler
(1957) in his theoretical explanations of the 60 compulsive
gamblers he analysed. The cornerstone of his theory was
the concept of masochism, which he defined in terms of
'an unconscious wish to lose'. Losing at gambling could
function in a variety of ways, as a penalty for attempting
to be omnipotent, punishment for parricidal feelings and
an alibi for the inner conscience. Anticipating loss provided a thrill that was sought for its pleasurable/painful
tension.

Additional themes have been added or emphasised.
Several writers have linked 'Lady Luck' with childhood
experiences with the mother. For Galdston (1960),
appeals to luck were in essence the gambler asking 'do you
love me?' Similar maternal themes were addressed by
Matussek (1953) and Ashton (1979) who hypothesised
that even the money used in gambling was symbolic of the
mother. Compulsive gambling has been interpreted as a
defence against depression and as an unsuccessful defence
against an underlying anal fixation, see Halliday and Fuller
(1974) who noted the images of the retention and expul-
sion of faeces associated with words such as 'craps' and
'the pot'. Adler (1966) proposed that gambling and
alcohol abuse were functionally equivalent; a parallel with
addictions drawn in all three other theoretical areas.

The central explanatory concepts of neurosis, sexual
tension, guilt and masochism have generally been
explored in the context of a compulsive gambler undergo-
ing psychoanalysis. These case reports fail to separate data
from interpretations. Greenberg (1980) suggested that
these hypotheses were not supported by the evidence.

Less than 20 per cent of gamblers entering treatment programmes were diagnosed as neurotic, few fitted the pattern of guilt and masochism, and sexual adjustment was generally good. In addition the failure to establish differences in personality between social, frequent and compulsive gamblers may further undermine psychoanalytic theorising. This, however, is debatable. The evidence has not been derived from research designed to specifically address analytic concepts pertaining to gambling. Statements concerning a general measure of 'sexual adjustment' may have no bearing on the themes of sexual tension and guilt incorporated in a psychoanalytic explanation of a single case. The problem encountered here is central to the scientific evaluation of psychoanalysis generally; as they are presently defined, psychoanalytic hypotheses have been considered to be untestable and irrefutable (Popper 1963).

Bergler (1957), like many other theorists, devoted time to the definition of compulsive gamblers: habitually takes chances, is full of optimism, experiences the thrill of pleasurable/painful tension. At least these characteristics were specified in terms of some observable state of the universe and are more readily evaluated. From the data reviewed earlier it can be seen that the idea that the compulsive gambler bets on anything whenever possible is quite inaccurate. In terms of the risk-taking aspects of personality, research has suggested that there are no differences between social, low-frequency gamblers and regular heavy punters. In addition, 23 per cent of compulsive gamblers used only one specific form of betting, i.e. their betting behaviour and risk-taking occurred in only a single type of gambling environment. Similarly, the notion of overwhelming optimism is too simplistic. Although the data supported the general trend for regular gamblers to be more optimistic about winning, some were quite presimistic about a particular bet.

Finally, on the topic of masochism, Bergler's (1957)

'wish to lose' has been evaluated by Oldman (1978) as an outsider's too simple summary of a variety of conflicting needs, expectations and beliefs:

1 Needing to win. The gambler may have no other means of repaying a debt.
2 Hoping to win.
3 Knowledge that there is the possibility not just of winning but of making a 'killing'.

These components comprise a sense of 'hopeless optimism' together with

4 The expectation of losing. This, after all, is how bookies and casinos make money.

Such an analysis of the inherent contradictions of the behaviour of persisting at gambling when losing is much more persuasive and open to research evaluation than 'an unconscious wish to lose'. The difference may well be a function of Oldman's first-hand experience of gambling and Bergler's knowledge derived only from gamblers in treatment.

Although psychoanalysis has neither contributed much to our understanding of gambling nor generated research, it is possible that concepts of development and unconscious processes may in the future play a part in explanations of the motivation of the so-called compulsive gambler. The sweeping generalisations based upon a single case may need to be tempered with the collection of some basic data. The literature does for some people have a certain energy and appeal: '. . . and in some ways, I am persuaded the gambler is right: for who can make up, and what can cancel out, the egregious loss of the mother's assuring love and the father's supportive sanction? Such a one is doomed to wander through life asking unanswerable questions.' (Galdston 1960.) Moran (1975a) in a review of the psychoanalytic textbook by Halliday and Fuller (1974) quoted the famous words of Lincoln: 'People who like this sort of thing will find this the sort of thing they like.'

Psychiatric explanations

Bolen and Boyd (1968) were instrumental in drawing the attention of psychiatrists, particularly in the US, to the problems of regular gamblers who sought help. Apart from endorsing psychoanalytic theorising they concluded that it was more appropriate to view 'pathological' gambling as a complex symptom to be found in a wide variety of psychiatric disorders rather than to diagnose it as a specific disorder in its own right. It will be seen in the course of the following review that the position is now reversed; pathological gambling is now defined as a separate impulse disorder.

Opinion in the US tends to the view that the causes of pathological gambling are obscure. Despite its epidemiological significance (*c.* 1.1 million pathological gamblers in the US) the syndrome has rarely been studied (Custer 1982; Greenberg 1980). Despite this obscurity, various important theoretical concepts have been formulated and merit attention. There are three main areas of theorising:

1 Definitions of 'social' as opposed to 'pathological' gambling. (Bolen & Boyd 1968; Moran 1975; Custer 1982; Greenberg 1980).
2 Types of pathological gambling (Moran 1975).
3 The resemblance of pathological gamblers to substance addicts, and related explanatory concepts (Moran 1970b, Custer 1982).

Definitions

All the psychiatric definitions have attempted to specify the characteristics of pathological gambling that distinguish it from the social, or normal variety. For Bolen and Boyd (1968) the former was typified by an 'excessive preoccupation with gambling and sustained significant economic losses'. It can be seen from the review of the descriptive data that these two variables fail to discriminate between gamblers entering treatment and habitual punters who do not want or seek help.

Moran (1970a, 1975) rejected the term 'compulsive' as

in his view gamblers failed to satisfy Lewis's (1936) criterion for compulsions: that the person finds his or her behaviour alien and tries to resist it. Pathological gambling was considered to be a syndrome in its own right, or secondary to some other psychiatric disorder. Moran's definition emphasised four general aspects; concern by the gambler or their family about the amount of gambling, the experience of an overpowering urge to gamble, loss of control once gambling had begun, and related disturbances in the life of the gambler. These themes have face-validity but they lack operational definition. In contrast, the diagnostic criteria for pathological gambling included in the American Psychiatric Association's latest classification of mental disorders, DSM-III (1980), contains a list of specific actions or events. These criteria were drafted by Custer.

Diagnostic criteria for Pathological Gambling
A. The individual is chronically and progressively unable to resist impulses to gamble.
B. Gambling compromises, disrupts or damages familial, personal, and vocational pursuits, as indicated by at least three of the following:
(1)   Arrest for forgery, fraud, embezzlement or income tax evasion due to attempts to obtain money for gambling;
(2)   default on debts or other financial responsibilities;
(3)   disrupted family or spouse relationships due to gambling;
(4)   borrowing of money from illegal sources (loan sharks);
(5)   inability to account for loss of money or to produce evidence of winning money if this is claimed;
(6)   loss of work due to absenteeism in order to pursue gambling activity;
(7)   necessity for another person to provide money to relieve a desperate financial situation.
C. The gambling is not due to Antisocial Personality Disorder. (American Psychiatric Association 1980: 291)

Spitzer and Williams (1980) defined the three strands that represented the objectives of the classification of mental disorders as embodied in DMS-III. They were communication, control (i.e. preventing the occurrence of, or modifying the course of, the disorder) and comprehension (i.e. understanding the causes). It appears that so far the first objective has been met by the inclusion of pathological gambling in DSM-III as it has resulted in an upsurge of interest and research (Custer 1982).

In addition to defining the abnormal, Greenberg (1980) proposed some identifying characteristics of the normal gambler. These were a desire for relaxation, profit motive, inherent pleasure in exercising a variety of ego-functions and the attraction of risk-taking. Likewise, Custer (1982) proposed that the social gambler can stop at any time, has no self-values associated with winning or losing, has other aspects of life that are more important and rewarding and, finally, rarely has a big win.

The psychiatric work on definitions has been entirely theoretical. The above attempts to distinguish between social and pathological gamblers, between normality and disorder, have not been validated. If the assumption is made that the universe of gamblers consists of two groups, punters who bet once a week or less and those who enter treatment, then the above definitions and the DSM-III criteria would have good face validity. However, direct observations in the real world of gambling suggested that there is a large number of gamblers in between these two groups. People gamble at all levels of frequency and stake size. The conclusion reached in the previous chapter was that gamblers who seek treatment are not readily distinguishable from any other habitual gamblers. It seemed more reasonable to view high-frequency gamblers as a single heterogeneous group who differed in the degree of self-control of their betting behaviour. Those attending treatment programmes (and called 'pathological' by psychiatrists), may be less likely to exhibit control than most (as they have somewhat larger debts and use larger stakes) but they do not form a distinct group. If this conclusion is substantiated by further research it undermines at least one of the fundamental assumptions of a classification system such as DSM-III. Spitzer and Williams (1980) specified three assumptions: (a) that there are individuals with 'relatively distinct and clinically significant behavioural syndromes. . . .'; (b) that the pattern of behaviour cause 'distress and disability'; and (c) 'that something is wrong with the person'. The empirical data concerning compulsive gamblers only provides some support for the second. One of the major criticisms of the DSM-III classification system itself is that given these three assumptions what behaviours could be excluded from 'mental disorder' (Schacht & Nathan 1977)? The significant social and political implications of this and other criticisms are beyond the scope of this book.

The extension of the rubric of mental disorder to encompass habitual gamblers has been based primarily on the apparent distinction between those who seek help and the assumed characteristics of the social gambler. In the United States in particular, several factors might conspire to produce this distinction: the selection bias inherent in studying those attending GA; the tiny number of treatment programmes; and most important of all, the lack of knowledge about high-frequency gamblers in general. It is only in such a context that one can reasonably evaluate the characteristics of those gamblers who seek help.

Typology

Moran (1970a) reported a preliminary investigation into the typology of pathological gamblers. Fifty gamblers referred for psychiatric help were allocated, on the basis of interviews with the gambler and, whenever possible, the next of kin, to one of five categories of pathological gambling:
1 subcultural
2 neurotic
3 impulsive
4 psychopathic
5 symptomatic

The categories were not considered to be mutually exclus-
ive and the author made it clear that allocation to one
category rather than another was decided by evaluating
the relative importance of the various factors, though how
this was done was not specified. General descriptions
rather than operational definitions of each category were
given and no attempt was made to examine the reliability
with which such categories might be used. One suspects
that Moran, like most others who have worked with gamblers who seek help, was struck by the heterogeneous
nature of such a group of people. In the absence of any
methodological or statistical analysis the report was clearly
speculative. No further research on the matter has been
published and yet Kusyszyn (1973) stated that 'as many as
five varieties of pathological gambling have been identified'. This was clearly wishful thinking.

Given the social and moral implications of the term
'psychopath' it was particularly unfortunate that Moran
linked this label with gambling without specifying the
diagnostic criteria he employed: 'In this case (i.e. variety
of pathological gambling) the basic abnormality was that
of psychopathy' (Moran 1970a). Similarly, Seager (1970)
reported that half of his group of treated gamblers showed
evidence of 'psychopathic traits', e.g. 'many jobs left for
trivial reasons', 'immature attitude to their predicament,
their family and their responsibilities'. Sixteen per cent of
psychiatrists surveyed in the UK considered that pathological gambling was associated with psychopathy, and this
view was significantly associated with a failure to recom-
mend any treatment (Dickerson 1974).

Recent advances in the definition of psychopathic
behaviour (Hare & Schalling 1978) provide a sounder
research methodology, should future studies explore the
relationship between gambling and psychopathy. However, in the absence of empirical data it may be helpful to
speculate on why some psychiatrists have felt justified in
using the diagnosis. A good starting point is Wray's (1980)
report that over 60 per cent of GA members thought that

they used to lie, not just to cover up gambling, but eventually quite gratuitously. That gamblers retain this habit when contacting helping agents seems likely and may account for the commonly reported difficulties in establishing a one-to-one therapeutic relationship (Bolen & Boyd 1968; Seager 1970; Custer 1982).

It is reasonable to suppose that it is not just the lying that triggers the term 'psychopath' but rather the perception that the gambler seems to be operating ouside a conventional moral framework. Even if one considers only the value system associated with money it is clear that some high-frequency gamblers view cash in an unusual way. Coins and notes or bills are described as 'gambling money, i.e. something you need in order to bet rather than something that pays the rent and feeds the family. Lies then become part of such a gambler's necessary isolation; how could he or she even tell a friend they were drawing out their savings to spend (lose) it on a poker machine? The gambler may operate within such a value system for many years. The meeting between a helping agent (e.g. a psychiatrist) and such a gambler, that eventually breaks the isolation, is unlikely to have been precipitated by the gambler's rejection of this unique value system but rather by another's discovery of it. Thus problems of communication are bound to occur; the psychiatrist thinking of 'stealing', remorse, shame and guilt, and the gambler of 'borrowing' and no feelings of remorse, etc.

Addiction and related concepts

Embedded in the detailed descriptions of gamblers, Custer (1982) included a variety of explanatory concepts. They were not articulated into a single theoretical model but most centre around the theme of addiction. Earlier Moran (1970a) had speculated that pathological gambling might be caused by 'a morbid type of psychological dependence'. Custer was struck by the extent to which the gamblers he encountered in treatment programmes and at

GA meetings resembled substance addicts. Pathological gambling was perhaps a drugless impulsive disorder with the potential to stimulate, tranquilise or even relieve pain. Custer noted that gambling could generate stress and tension but also subjective feelings of importance and power. On further stress, especially following losing, it was hypothesised that a person gambled again to have access to these feelings. In some unspecified way, euphoria on winning and the pleasure of the gambling activity itself (he uses Goffman's (1967a) 'the action') maintain this cycle of events. This aspect of Custer's theorizing is disjointed and in no way clarified by the introduction of yet another concept, an intense unconscious or consciously suppressed fear of death. This interest in thanatophobia was shared by Greenberg (1980) but is purely speculative.

Despite the lack of clarity of definition, the central theoretical theme of pathological gambling as an addiction-like phenomenon is supported by some of the available data. Loss of control, escalation of stake size and 'cold turkey' experiences following sudden cessation of high-frequency gambling have all found limited support. Furthermore, in their manner of referral to psychiatric centres gamblers share some of the characteristics of those who drink excessively or are addicted to other substances (Dickerson 1977a). Often the referral has been initiated by relatives, friends or probation officers, etc., on behalf of the gambler and at this time he or she is often personally and socially isolated. Although it may well be valid and heuristic to draw parallels between gambling and other addictions, as yet psychiatric theorising has not produced a model open to evaluative research.

Sociological explanations

For Oldman (1978) the compulsive gambler was like the yeti, much spoken of but rarely seen. While working in a casino for two years he noted that only one customer had ever been described as 'compulsive'; a man who played roulette in the few remaining hours before a court appearance for non-payment of a debt. Oldman, in contrast to other casino staff, found this man's actions quite rational: it represented his only hope of avoiding a prison sentence. This theme is similar to Lesieur's (1979) hypothesis regarding the compulsive gambler's belief that it was 'correct' to chase. However, both these sociologists have very different starting points, Oldman with casino regulars and Lesieur mainly with gamblers who had sought help from GA. Their theoretical contributions are complementary and it is perhaps best to consider them in turn.

The comparative rarity with which the label 'compulsive' was used in the casino settting formed the starting point for Oldman's hypothesis that compulsive gambling was essentially a problem of the sociology of knowledge. That is to say, its coinage and usage was a function of the relationship between 'patient' (a gambler in trouble through betting) and 'doctor' (psychiatrist, psychologist, probation officer, etc.) and the lack of knowledge of the 'doctor' regarding habitual gambling. Oldman considered, reasonably, that two years' observation of habitual gamblers at the roulette tables placed him in a position of sufficient knowledge to propose the following sequence of variables and events:

1 The availability of casino facilities.
2 The choice of some to be regular customers.
3 The possibility of a financial crisis.

Only at the last point, when it had already become accepted, either by the gambler or more often by some significant other, that 'something must be done', did the compulsive gambler 'appear'. According to Oldman's hypothesis, he or she 'appeared' simply by what he called 'the adoption of the rhetoric of compulsion'. Thus for Oldman there were only habitual (or high-frequency) gamblers, some of whom had encountered a financial crisis. If one added 'and sometimes related personal, employment and legal problems' then it can be concluded that Oldman's position is very much in agreement with the conclusions reached in the previous chapter; that compulsive gamblers do not seem to be different from most high-frequency gamblers and that the name is a function of their seeking help.

Oldman analysed the relationship between habitual gambling and the possibility of a financial crisis. He noted the need for regular customers to have a certain way of life to permit late and long hours to be spent in the casino, together with the type of work that gave access to regular amounts of cash. In addition it required economic arrangements that were capable of withstanding quite massive fluctuations in expenditure. Using an example of a hypothetical customer prepared to spend on average in the long term about £5 ($10) per night, this would involve staking about £50 ($100) per night (Oldman assumed on the basis of his observations that the casino in which he worked took about 10 per cent per night of a customer's money stake). Some nights the gambler might win a little, occasionally might have a bonanza, but this would be matched by those weeks when all was lost: £350 ($700). Thus, without involving any concept of loss of control, Oldman was able to indicate that a financial crisis was a probability unless the habitual gambler had extra realisable resources and tolerant creditors.

Oldman's pragmatic conclusion was that the mechanism whereby a gambler reached a crisis point, sought help and hence accepted the label 'compulsive', was not a consequence of some personality defect 'but of a defective relationship between a strategy of play on one hand and of managing one's finances on the other'. This view of habitual gambling fails to account for the self-reported experience of loss of control, of spending more than was planned, of losing all cash-in-hand. Oldman discussed the concept of compulsion and argued that the term only became salient after it had been accepted that there was a problem and that something had to be done about the gambling behaviour. Loss of control cannot be dealt with in the same way. It is reported by regular gamblers who do not express a need to stop or reduce their gambling, who do not consider they have a problem.

Lesieur's (1979) theorising seems more traditional, starting with an attempt to define the compulsive gambler: 'the acquisition of the chase philosophy is the major contingency in becoming a compulsive gambler'. Non-compulsive gamblers who had lost money viewed chasing, betting more money the next day, as stupid. However, for the compulsive gambler it was logical and the correct way to bet. Lesieur supposed that the underlying reasoning was that it had worked in the past, it was giving oneself a chance to get even, and other gamblers got out of trouble that way.

Despite the empirical data that suggested that most high-frequency gamblers (and even some low-frequency ones) know the experience of wanting to chase, and probably chased to a greater or lesser extent, there is at present no evidence that at some point some high-frequency gamblers come to believe that chasing is correct. It seems more likely that Lesieur based this hypothesis on the experiences of gamblers in extreme situations similar to that described by Oldman at the beginning of this section. The belief is not so much a belief in chasing but rather a belief that a large sum of money has to be obtained by the next day, or whenever. Once a gambler believes he must obtain this money, and at times such thinking would be quite understandable in terms of possible loss of job, prison sentence or violence, then it follows quite logically that further gambling is the only possible way of achieving such an objective – apart, that is, from robbing a bank.

We can now turn our attention to the most convincing aspect of Lesieur's analysis of what he termed the gamblers 'spiral of options'. In order to finance their gambling he hypothesised that the compulsive gambler carried out a series of actions perceived by him as ranging from the moral to the immoral.

As the actions carried out to obtain money became more immoral the gambler's ability to justify them was

Table 5.1 Lesieur's (1979) 'spiral of options' experienced by the gambler in search of money

Actions	Perceived morality	Justification
1 Hustling at pool etc. Bookmaking Loans from friends Use of loan sharks 'Borrowing' from accounts at work Petty larceny	Totally moral	By belief or situation: 'People expect to be hustled'; 'Everybody does it'
2. Forging cheques 'Assisting' in burglary	Partially immoral	Partly justifiable and excuses
3 Bank robbery	Immoral	Excuses only: 'I had to pay the rent'; 'They were going to kill me'

increasingly replaced by excuses. In Lesieur's group only five out of fifty gamblers proceeded to the stage of robbing a bank or some similar act. This theoretical schema provides some explanation of the apparently incredible figures noted earlier regarding the duration of gambling at a problem level: five or more years. In addition, the description of the gambler slowly and remorselessly running out of options whereby finances can be obtained provides a possible framework for further research, particularly if the objective is to estimate the indirect costs to society of habitual gambling.

Psychological explanations

Theories explaining persistence at gambling under conditions of financial loss have commonly been derived from behavioural theories on intermittent reinforcement. The review below focuses on this work and also includes two relevant explanatory concepts from abnormal psychology: theories of compulsive behaviours and the 'behaviour completion mechanism' (McConaghy 1980).

Behavioural theories

In all respects Skinner's (1953) choice of the term 'pathological' to describe gambling was unfortunate. Although he was clearly referring to the situation where gambling was frequent and continued despite heavy losses, the illness connotations of the term were a contradiction of his proposal that the behaviour was a function of the contingencies of the gambling environment. Skinner gave no explicit descriptions but proposed that this pathological behaviour was a result of variable ratio (VR) reinforcement schedules. A wide range of animal laboratory studies had established that steady high rates of responding could be maintained by quite infrequent rewards (Ferster & Skinner 1957). Gambling situations were assumed to be similar to the animal laboratory, with the reinforcement of a cash win being relatively infrequent yet sufficient to develop and maintain gambling until a pathological level was reached, when, 'the utility is negative and the gambler loses all' (Skinner 1972).

The earliest experimental studies to examine the relationship between partial schedules of reinforcement and persistence when losing were completed by Lewis and Duncan (1956, 1957, 1958) using a poker machine. Subjects experienced a simple two-stage paradigm of playing and winning on a percentage of pulls (the training period) and then continuing playing without winning at all until they decided to stop (the extinction period). Subjects persisted longer during extinction when they had won less frequently during training. Persistence also increased when larger amounts were won. These studies, in spite of the use of a poker machine, were quite unrealistic. Subjects were given unlimited supplies of tokens to play the machine and the ratios of 'winning' (33, 67, and 100%) were much higher than would be experienced in real life. (Scarne (1975) calculated that the 'Twenty-One Bell' three-reeler, when set to give a 95 per cent return, gave a win of some kind on about 13 per cent of pulls.)

The laboratory study by Levitz (1971) was more satisfactory. The subjects were the inevitable male undergraduates who were paid 1.30 dollars per hour for participation and in the gambling game could lose this money as well as any accumulated winnings. The 'gamble' was a laboratory game involving the problem of predicting which of four lamps would next light up. In a training period of twenty-two trials, subjects either won one dollar on VR 36 per cent or lost one dollar on VR 14 per cent. Subjects then could choose to continue the game for up to a further fifty-one trials on the losing schedule of VR 14 per cent. Those who had won during training persisted significantly longer in this second stage. Subjects were also given feedback during the training stage; they were told they were predicting better than other people, about the same, or worse. Levitz concluded that a subject's perception of doing better than others was as important in producing persistence as the winning of money. If this can be generalised to real-life gambling, 'beginner's luck' may be less important than a gambler's belief that he or she was a winner when beginning gambling. This study also illustrated another cognitive factor, later to be called the 'illusion of control' (Langer 1975), i.e. the more subjects perceived the game as skill-determined the longer they persisted when losing.

Even with studies as well designed as Levitz's, the gap between the laboratory and the real world is enormous. Is it possible to generalise from behaviour over 51 trials to the 1,077 consecutive bets at roulette observed by Hochauer (1970)? What if the period of persisting despite losing extends over many years?

The efforts of behaviourists to overcome this gap have resulted in what is commonly referred to as the experimental analysis of behaviour. This is best summarised in terms of the temporal sequence

$$S_D \text{------} R \text{------} S_{R+}$$

i.e. the discriminative stimulus (S_D), the response (R) and the reinforcement (S_{R+}). This analysis, especially when applied to complex human behaviour in natural environments, is wholly dependent upon the concise definition of the response (R) being studied. Having defined the response, observations are made of the stimulus conditions (S_D) that prevail just prior to the response and those that occur or alter immediately after (S_{R+}). Nothing need be assumed about the nature of the reinforcement except that it is more effective the closer in time that it follows a response. The objective is to discover all the variables of which the probability of a response may be a function. Although this appears an impossible goal the experimental analysis of behaviour has proved a valuable and flexible method of studying human behaviour in real environments (Haynes & Wilson 1979).

Applied to gambling (see, for example, Knapp 1976) the response might be defined in terms of behaviours such as placing chips on the roulette table, shaking and rolling

Table 5.2 'Blower' stimulus chain for dog and horse races

Stimulus DOGS	Repetitions dogs	Time before 'Off' (mins)	Stimulus HORSES	Repetitions horses	Time before 'Off' (mins)
1. They're parading	1	9–13	They're parading – They all go at – The runners at –	1	15–20
2. They bet at – 6/4 trap 2, etc.	3	0–4	They bet at 6/4 parsimony, etc.	8–15	0–16
3. They're going in	1	0–2	They're going down	1	5–8
4. The hare's running	1	3–5 sec	They're at the start	1	1–5
5. —	1	—	They're going behind They're in the stalls	1	1–2
6. —	—	—	They're under orders	1	0–1
7. THEY'RE OFF!	0	0	THEY'RE OFF!	0	0

the dice, passing cash and a betting slip across the take counter, pulling the lever of a poker machine, etc. In most gambling environments the repetitive nature of the game commonly produced a regular sequence of antecedent stimuli such as clearing the table, payout, calling for bets, spinning the wheel, rolling the ball and 'no more bets'. Table 5.2 summarises the typical sequence of announcements on the 'blower' – the commentary relayed from the racecourse – in off course betting offices in the UK (Dickerson 1979).

If attention is now turned to what happens immediately after a betting response, depending on the form of gambling there is the rolling of the dice, spinning of a wheel or reels, the running of the race, etc. The duration of these events varies from a few seconds in roulette and poker machines to many minutes in horse-race betting. At this point Skinner's (1953, 1972) assumption that cash delivered on a VR schedule was the reinforcement for gambling seems somewhat inaccurate. In the laboratory when food-deprived animals on VR schedules are reinforced, a food pellet is delivered immediately; there is no delay. The delay between the betting response and cash won (or lost) poses problems for a behavioural account of persisting at gambling when losing. Montgomery and Kreitzer (1968) attempted to overcome this with the hypothesis that the betting response was immediately followed by the anticipation of winning'. Although the evidence is scant it seems unlikely that high-frequency gamblers have some thought or image of winning at such a moment, but rather that their attention is focused on the stimulus events that are occurring: the rolling dice, the race commentary, etc.

Let it be supposed that this period of stimulus events is reinforcing to some gamblers. Early in a person's experience, betting responses might occur with great variability at any time prior to the onset of this reinforcing event. Behavioural theory would predict that the betting responses closer to the onset of reinforcement would be more strongly reinforced and their probability of recurring would rise in relation to those responses earlier in the time sequence. Thus the frequency of late betting responses would increase and earlier responses would decay. Very experienced gamblers would therefore appear to gamble in a very regular pattern. Their betting responses would show little temporal variability and would commonly occur in association with those stimuli that signal the onset of reinforcement, e.g. 'no more bets', 'they're off'.

There is some evidence to suggest that regular or high-frequency gamblers do in fact show this kind of gambling behaviour and that this is one way in which they differ from low-frequency gamblers. As noted in the previous chapter, regular roulette players commonly place their chips late, once the ball has been released and as the call of 'no more bets' is occurring. Whether or not this late staking is associated with cognitions based on strategies of beating the croupier (Oldman 1974) does not undermine the prediction based on the efficacy of reinforcement. It

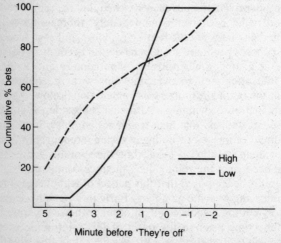

Fig. 2   Comparison of the cumulative percentage bets placed per minute by high and low-frequency gamblers (*Source*: Journal of Applied Behavior Analysis 1979, **12**, 315–23.)

is the temporal contiguity of response and reinforcement that is all-important.

There is rather firmer evidence for late bet placement in high-frequency off-course betting in the UK, where the race commentary is broadcast. This is illustrated in Figure 2 (Dickerson 1979).

It is tempting to speculate from a behavioural viewpoint that poker machines are most efficiently designed; the structure of the machine itself ensures that the lever pull is invariably timed to occur just prior to the hypothesised reinforcement of the spinning reels. The importance of giving the player a 'good spin' for their money and balancing this against the needs of the owner to have as many pulls per unit time as possible, is well recognised and researched by the designers of new machines. For example, as fourth and fifth reels have been introduced the machines have been designed to have the reels spin for exactly the same total time as the earlier three-reelers. The only way in which a player can enhance the available reinforcement might be to play several machines at once and this is exactly what some high-frequency players do. This may increase persistence as other behaviours, such as feeding the coin and moving between machines, become more strongly reinforced.

It seems reasonable to conclude that there is some support for the suggestion that the stimulus events, such as reels spinning, race commentaries, etc., act as reinforcers of the betting behaviour of some regular gamblers. The experimental analysis of behaviour does not provide information concerning the subjective experience of the reinforcement. However, from the descriptive data already reviewed it seems likely that it is during the reinforcing stimulus events in question that some gamblers have the most intense experiences of excitement, arousal and tension. Such observations have yet to explored and validated empirically. However, the self-reports of changes in physiological arousal experienced during gambling have been one of the main reasons why persistence at gambling despite losing has been considered to be an addictive pattern of behaviour. Wray and Dickerson (1981) found tentative support for such a view, finding positive correlations between self-reports of the level of excitement experienced while betting, the number of withdrawal-like symptoms following ceasing to gamble, and the degree of difficulty experienced when trying to give up gambling. Another implication for persistence within any particular session would be the cost of stopping, i.e. the loss to the gambler of access to the reinforcing stimulus events. In addition, for the gambler at crisis point, this might also involve a return to aversive situations: angry creditors, estranged family and the opportunity to worry about such problems.

The experimental analysis of behaviour applied to gambling has thus generated the proposal that at least two main forms of reinforcement operate to shape up and maintain betting responses; cash, and the excitement associated with the stimulus events of the particular form of gambling. It has been suggested that these reinforcers act together in a conjunctive schedule involving both ratio and temporal aspects (Dickerson 1974, 1979). This proposal has been found wanting in several important respects in an appraisal by Saunders and Wookey (1978), but contemporary theories of conditioning may well be a source of heuristic models of the reinforcement schedules operating in gambling environments (see, for example, Logan 1979).

A learning process is essentially dynamic but there are no data documenting the development over time of higher frequencies of betting responses in individual gamblers. The following sequence of training is a more detailed version of one proposed earlier to account for the development of high-frequency gambling in off-course betting offices (Dickerson 1979b):

1   Low-frequency betting with multiple bets placed out of racing hours or on the day prior to the races; regular small cash wins.

2 Opportunity to bet and stay in the office (non-working days, unemployment, shifts, absence of other leisure activities); single win or each-way bets and listening to the race commentary – both cash and 'excitement' reinforcement shape up further responses and staying longer. Ending the session begins to involve the response cost of losing access to reinforcing events.

3 Betting responses become more frequent, staking occurs as late as possible before the off and is predictably associated with the cycle of stimulus events.

4 Stake size escalates – larger bets are more strongly reinforced both by greater excitement and sometimes by larger wins; 'excitement' habituates after many repetitions; diffuse social pressures to use larger stakes when betting at the last moment when others are watching and staff may have to process the bet after the 'off'.

5 'Training' may be said to be complete when the person is regularly betting whenever time and money permit and when cash itself becomes an S_D to bet, i.e. it becomes 'gambling money'.

6 Debts incurred may act as 'deprivation' and lead to increased frequencies of betting when money becomes available.

Prospective longitudinal data are required to evaluate such a sequence and also to examine the part played by other factors such as cognitions and mood. The social learning concept of self-efficacy (Bandura 1977) would suggest that cognitive factors such as the perception of betting as a skilful task, learning from the models provided by other gamblers, expecting to win and believing that one's performance is better than others, may all play a part in the early stages of changing from a low to a high frequency of betting. However, it is difficult to provide a persuasive cognitive or rational account of high-frequency betting and losing when the behaviour persists over many years.

Psychological explanation of compulsive behaviour

The repeated meticulous washing of hands, the laborious making and re-making of beds, etc., seem far removed from the regular playing of roulette or betting with a bookie. There are, however, sufficient similarities to justify a brief consideration of the theoretical explanations of compulsions.

A person who completes a compulsive ritual, for example to save their spouse from being killed, may when away from the situation perceive the irrational nature of what they do and express a wish to stop the behaviour. Yet on return home the same person may experience the urge to carry out the behaviour and will repetitively complete the specific ritual. Urges may occur 'out of the blue' or be precipitated by some stimulus or event and may be accompanied by strong feelings of discomfort or anxiety. The behaviour may take up several hours of each day, have a deleterious impact on all aspects of daily living, may escalate at times of stress and may persist for many years. Mowrer (1956) considered that compulsions were a prime example of the 'neurotic paradox'.

In broad terms the parallel with persistence at gambling despite losing is that compulsive behaviours are repetitive, time-consuming behaviours that persist despite the costs incurred. The central concept invoked to explain compulsive behaviour has been anxiety reduction (Foa & Steketee 1979; Rachman & Hodgson 1980). Both clinical reports and observations, and empirical studies of physiological parameters such as heart-rate and skin conductance, provide support for the following sequence: the urge to carry out the behaviour, a rapid rise in subjective discomfort (plus related physiological events) and the repeated completion of the behaviour associated with a partial reduction of the discomfort. When a person is prevented from carrying out the compulsive act the discomfort rapidly peaks and then slowly decays; more slowly than during the compulsive behaviour. Similar discomfort and autonomic arousal has been reported for compulsive gamblers when, as a part of treatment, they have been exposed to poker machines in a club but not permitted to play (Blaszczynski 1982). However, an anxiety reduction concept does not seem to fit with the other empirical data or with the proposal in the previous section that the very process of gambling may be exciting or arousing particularly for those who bet frequently and persist when losing. There are few observations that a session of gambling may be calming or anaesthetising.

Behaviour completion mechanism (BCM)

In a theoretical review of the possible mechanisms underlying the effects of psychological treatments for problems such as agoraphobia, specific phobias and unwanted sexual orientation, McConaghy (1980) described a neurophysiological intervening variable, the behaviour completion mechanism (BCM). This was derived from the work of the physiologist Anokhin (1955) and reflected the Russian's interest in brain-behaviour correlates. The assumption made is that for every habitual behaviour there is a matching cortical model. This is activated by stimuli associated with the onset of the behaviour pattern and acts to inhibit general arousal, so facilitating the completion of the behaviour sequence. If, however, the behaviour is prevented, inhibition does not occur and arousal results. BCM's are supposed to account for the mild arousal experienced in delays occurring in everyday life such as waiting at traffic lights or in queues at checkouts.

Neurophysiological models of this kind are particularly difficult to evaluate in respect of human behaviour although in some research areas they have proved valuable. For example, similar models have been proposed for social and language development in children (Vygotsky 1962; Luria 1961, 1969) and have contributed to the growth of cognitive-behavioural techniques used to help children with learning problems (Meichenbaum and Asarnow 1979).

McConaghy (1980), however, added a further dimension to the BCM, proposing mechanisms by which two different psychological treatments, aversion thereapy and desensitization, had equivalent effects. His theory was derived from a series of studies of the treatment of homosexual patients (McConaghy 1969, 1970; McConaghy, Proctor & Barr 1972) and forms the theoretical model for the treatment programme for compulsive gamblers currently being completed at the University of New South Wales in Australia. McConaghy selected gambling as a behaviour which involved no primary drive but was, he thought, driven solely by the BCM: gambling should 'respond well to either systematic desensitization or aversion therapy' (McConaghy 1980: 150). In fact the preliminary results (McConaghy *et al.* 1982) showed that desensitization was significantly more effective in reducing both gambling behaviour and urges to gamble and yet the authors concluded that their results supported the existence of BCMs. In addition the face validity of the model is poor if the function of the BCM is to facilitate calm completion of gambling activities; as concluded previously, a subjective experience of excitement (and a physiological state of high autonomic arousal) may well be an integral part of habitual gambling.

Conclusions

Most of the theoretical explanations of compulsive gambling have been speculative rather than linked with any empirical research. Thus, particularly in the areas of psychoanalysis and psychiatry, there are a plethora of concepts but little or no supporting data. The review has emphasised the value of the work of Oldman (1978) in reducing the need for concepts of mental disorder by spelling out the realities of habitual gambling. Most of the research exploring the persistence of gambling despite losing has been based on the behaviour theory concepts of partial reinforcement schedules. The finding that some high-frequency gamblers bet as late as possible in the gambling cycle has been interpreted within the behavioural framework as an indication that certain stimulus events such as the race commentary, the spinning reels, etc., act as reinforcement, possibly associated with a subjective experience of excitement and raised levels of autonomic arousal.

Chapter 6

How do they stop or regain control?

Introduction

In attempting to provide answers to the question posed in the chapter heading, the main thrust of the discussion will involve the evaluation of studies that describe the treatment or help offered to gamblers by psychiatrists and psychologists and by specialist agencies such as Gamblers Anonymous. The aim is to draw out from treatment programmes those features that appear to be effective.

In Chapter 4 it was noted that despite the application, helpfully in some circumstances, of the label 'compulsive' to gamblers in treatment or attending GA, this carried no guarantee that they were uniquely different from any other group of gamblers who bet at a high frequency. If treated gamblers are much like any other high-frequency gambler, then effective treatment methods should be relevant to any person who wishes to reduce or stop his or her gambling behaviour. If this is so it is reasonable to expect that there will be similarities between effective treatments, the methods of control used by professional gamblers, and the means by which untreated high-frequency gamblers resolve their own problems of control. The evidence from the latter two groups is scanty but will be included to ensure that the discussion moves away from the jargon of a medical/psychological model to the everyday situation of a person gambling frequently and experiencing difficulties of control. This is emphasised in Chapter 7 in the form of a practical guide for such a person.

Abstinence or control?

To the person who uses hundreds of dollars or pounds for a single bet the question whether he or she would prefer to stop gambling altogether, or rather learn to reduce and control their betting, may seem absurdly academic. If large debts have already been incurred there may be no choice but to stop. Additionally the image of betting two or three dollars or pounds may seem ludicrous to the gambler and remote from the action they have previously enjoyed.

The question, however, is worthy of attention and, as Orford (1974) pointed out, those working in research and therapy concerning gamblers might well have a good deal to learn from the literature on alcoholism and alcohol abuse on the topic of treatment goals. A brief history of this contentious issue underlines the point. In 1969, regarding treatment goals for alcoholism the view of the US National Institute of Mental Health was that no alcoholic could ever learn to drink moderately, and that statements to the contrary were unwise and dangerous (Marlatt 1979). This then was the prescribed wisdom, but within ten years the situation had altered radically. The so called 'Rand Report' (Armor, Polich & Stambul 1978) found that only 10 per cent of alcoholics treated in abstinence-oriented centres remained dry during the 18-month follow-up period. Furthermore, 26 per cent of the treated alcoholics reported drinking in moderation. The issue is still not settled despite the numerous documented accounts of controlled drinking by former alcoholics (for a review of these studies see Pattison, Sobell and Sobell 1977). Here the concern is not so much with the emotive issue of 'one drink, one drunk' and whether abstinence is a 'better' goal than controlled drinking but what happened in the area of treatment research. The result was a rich vein of new treatments derived mainly from social learning theory and consisting of procedures designed to help alcoholics learn to moderate and control their drinking (Sobell & Sobell 1978; Chaney, O'Leary & Marlatt 1978; Caddy, Addington & Perkins 1978).

It has been pointed out previously (Dickerson 1974) that the goals of treating compulsive gamblers had not been discussed. At that time much of the treatment work seemed implicitly to accept that cessation of gambling was the obvious goal. Peck and Ashcroft (1972) may have been the exception when they reported that for one of the five gamblers treated by them, gambling 'ceased to be a major problem . . . did resume gambling, but only in a minor way'. Since then, Dickerson and Weeks (1979) explored in a single case study the issue of whether controlled gambling could be successfully acquired by a compulsive gambler. Some contemporary treatment programmes for gamblers in the US and Australia seem to view a controlled, usually reduced, level of gambling as an acceptable treatment goal (Politzer and Morrow 1980; Blaszczynski 1982) although as yet there are no descriptions of procedures designed specifically to achieve such a goal.

Returning to the starting point of the gambler using very high stakes, it is of interest to speculate on the different factors that would be likely to influence the selection of a treatment objective. Sometimes a gambler may express a preference for either abstinence or control; almost half the group treated by Blaszczynski *et al.* (1982) preferred a reduced, controlled level of expenditure. The habitual use of very high stakes together with the presence of large debts might suggest that abstinence has to be the treatment objective. Another factor might well be the opportunity in the gambling environment for some alternative behaviours. In a social club, such as the 'leagues clubs' in Australia, controlled use of poker machines might be achieved by the gambler learning to maintain other social activities with family and friends. In gambling environments that preclude, often by law, any activity except gambling, such as betting offices in the UK and Australia, controlled levels of gambling might only be achieved by avoiding remaining in the environment – entering, placing a bet and leaving – or by rigorous controls on the availability of cash.

Given the fact that in countries where gambling is legalised over 80 per cent of the adult population participates, then ceasing to bet may be as tough a goal for the gambler to achieve as abstinence for the alcoholic. As the availability of opportunities to gamble increases it would seem more appropriate to help gamblers maintain control, either by involvement in those types of gambling that do not seem to be addictive – pools, sweeps and so on – or by learning strategies that help maintain control in potentially addictive betting environments such as casinos and betting offices.

The importance of setting goals appropriate to the treatment programme was illustrated by the extreme discomfort experienced by members of a GA group when one of their number, a policeman, whose career was in jeopardy from any further 'falls' or 'busts', reported over a period of weeks a variety of successful bets culminating in antepost betting on the Boat Race. This was an example of controlled, planned betting usually alien to the compulsive gambler and certainly not appreciated in a group working toward the goal of total abstinence.

Approaches to helping compulsive gamblers

Psychoanalytic treatment

In 1968 Bolen and Boyd wrote that psychoanalysis, or variants of it, was the most frequently used treatment for compulsive gamblers, 'and the success rate is reportedly quite high'. Since that time there have been no further reports of the use of this form of treatment with gamblers. None the less, the work referred to by Bolen and Boyd merits a brief evaluation.

The literature consists of a number of case studies (Lindner 1950; Matussek 1953; Greenson 1947; Harris 1964) and the monumental work by Bergler (1957) describing the treatment of sixty gamblers. This was, and remains today, the largest reported group of gamblers treated by any method. This work is none the less difficult to evaluate as the majority of the data are inextricably entwined in a discussion of psychoanalytic theory. As this aspect of Bergler's work has already been considered, the purpose here is to examine the results of this method of helping gamblers. Of the 60 who entered analysis 15 (25% of the total) discontinued within six weeks. Thirty-three received an analysis of their 'whole neurosis' and all but 3 were described as cured. (The remaining 12 received treatment for their betting behaviour only). The success rate was, therefore, of the order of 50 per cent.

Despite the size of this group, Bergler was working at a time prior to the development of major studies into the effectiveness of psychoanalysis (Bergin 1971). His work is essentially a collection of case studies without any formal structure or measurement of outcome. Bolen and Boyd (1968) noted that the course of such therapy with gamblers was arduous, with frequent relapses and what they called 'secondary complications' (i.e. financial and legal problems!). To the commonsense view, minus the language of psychoanalytic theory, these would seem to be both the likely reasons why the gambler sought help and priority targets for problem solving.

Such a credibility gap between therapist and gambler at the outset, together with the financial burden of the treatment itself, would be sufficient to cause early termination by many. However, for those who remain in therapy, analysis could well be a process, however inefficient, by which the gambler could become more aware of the relationship between negative mood states and a return to gambling.

This relationship has been reported by Cummings, Gordon and Marlatt (1980). This is speculation and not an argument in support of the efficacy of psychoanalysis. Rachman and Wilson (1980) state at the conclusion of a lengthy and meticulous review of the status of psycho-analytic therapy: 'There is still no acceptable evidence to support the view that psychoanalysis is an effective treat-ment.' There are certainly no grounds for recommending that a gambler who wants to cease betting should enter psychoanalysis.

Psychiatric treatment

At a GA meeting in Australia, Peter, a young business-man, described his experiences of psychiatric care. When his business had collapsed and the full extent of his gam-bling debts could no longer be hidden from his wife he sought help from his general practitioner; he expressed his need in terms of wanting time to help pull himself together. He agreed to be admitted to a psychiatric unit. In his story he spoke first of the psychiatrist reaching for a textbook with the comment that he had not met one of these before, and then of the electric shocks given to his head. When the proposal was put to him that a psychol-ogist would now give shocks to his fingers he decided enough was enough and discharged himself.

For the purposes of this discussion the moral of this case illustration is that the separation of psychological from psychiatric treatments serves the convenience of this text and in no way contradicts the fact that both professions have played their part in the darker side of the history of psychiatric care by doing alien and sometimes unjustifi-able things to gamblers in the name of treatment. In this section the objective is to explore and evaluate the impact of traditional psychiatric treatment methods, such as drugs, electroconvulsive therapy, individual and group psychotherapy, on the problems of compulsive gamblers.

Despite an editorial in the British Medical Journal in 1968 which questioned whether gamblers should be offered treatment (perhaps a vain attempt to arrest the trend of incorporating all deviant and antisocial behaviours into the concept of mental illness) it is clear that both inpatient and outpatient psychiatric services have been used in the treatment of compulsive gamblers (Moran 1970a, 1975; Bolen 1974; Custer 1982). There are, however, no controlled studies or treatment outcome evaluations in the literature.

In the US Bolen and Boyd (1968) played an influential role in educating their colleagues regarding the understanding and treatment of compulsive gamblers. Although they were pessimistic about the effectiveness of psychiatric treatment, their evaluation seemed to be based on the theoretical assumption that gamblers seeking help evidenced severe personality disorders (an assumption that, as we have seen, has little support) rather than upon any empirical data concerning treatment outcome. The only report in the literature at that time was a single case study by Ling and Buckman (1963) in which the gambler was treated with a combination of supportive psychotherapy and drugs (LSD and methylphenidate). Despite the latter pharmacological cocktail, the authors reported cessation of gambling at six-months follow-up.

If this case typified the *ad hoc* approach to treating gamblers then Bolen and Boyd encouraged a trend toward individual and group psychotherapy (and, as we have seen above, the use of psychoanalysis) and in 1970 reported the results of a group therapy approach involving the spouses of gamblers together with the patient gambler (8 couples in all). After twenty-two months the results were that gambling was reduced in five and absent in three. The only other case reported in the literature at this time was by Victor and Krug (1967) who used 'paradoxical intention' in the context of individual psychotherapy. The patient was instructed to carry out an agreed programme of betting; the treatment was successful in stopping gambling.

In the UK Moran has been the most influential figure on the psychiatric scene and has been associated with a somewhat different trend in the development of treatment. He too played an important part in educating professional groups involved in psychiatric care with descriptive articles exploring possible clinical systems of classifying gamblers. His theoretical position was very similar to that of Bolen and Boyd (1968); gambling was assumed to be either primary or symptomatic of another problem, most commonly of a depressive state. In the latter case he recommended the use of tricyclic antidepressants or electro-convulsive therapy, followed by psychotherapy. In the early 1970s in the UK gamblers in the primary group became the focus for research into the effectiveness of behaviour modification, mainly aversion therapy. A survey of psychiatrists found that 40 per cent recommended behaviour therapy (half of those specified aversion therapy) as the treatment of choice for compulsive gamblers (Dickerson 1974).

Although the behaviour therapy work is reviewed in the next section, it is interesting to speculate on why UK gamblers in psychiatric care were subjected to aversion therapy faradic shocks whereas there are no reports of a similar approach being adopted in the US. Certainly, in both countries there was a rapid development of interest in behaviour modification (Rimm & Masters 1979) and in aversion therapy specifically (Rachman & Teasdale 1969). There is the possibility that the legalisation of betting offices throughout the UK in 1960 had the effect of (i) leading some confirmed regular gamblers more rapidly into a financial crisis and related problems by providing more opportunity to gamble, and (ii) making it easier for these gamblers to seek and to be offered professional help since gambling was no longer illegal. Even a relatively small number of a new type of patient arriving in the psychiatric centres of a public health service in a geographically small country may have been noticed, resulting in a brief burst of activity among researchers seeking an appropriate treatment. That aversion therapy was chosen was not surprising as at that time it was being used on other so-called anti-social or deviant behaviours, such as sexual disorders and alcoholism (Rachman & Teasdale 1969).

In contrast, in the US, gambling of a potentially addictive nature would be enjoyed locally but illegally, or legally in Las Vegas itself. Both conditions might conspire to make it difficult for gamblers to seek help from public agencies and there would be but a few who could afford private therapy, most likely in the form of psychotherapy or psychoanalysis. Whatever the truth of the matter it was not until the mid-1970s, in both countries, that progress was made in the development of psychiatric treatment approaches specifically geared to the needs of compulsive gamblers.

In the UK the origins of the change were to be found in a small multi-disciplinary group of people involved in psychiatric care, the helping agencies generally and GA, later to be founder members of the Society for the Study of Gambling. The discussions and deliberations of this group resulted in a *Guide* (Dickerson 1975) edited by a committee that included key figures in the development of services for compulsive gamblers, namely Gordon Moody and Emmanuel Moran. The objective was to inform helping agencies about how to assist gamblers with their problems and thereby shift the availability of specialist help away from psychiatric centres. The content of this report took the form of a practical guide and although based on the author's training and experience in behaviour modification was written in a non-technical manner, emphasised specific problem-directed actions that a compulsive gambler might take, and commended the use of GA. Although this *Guide* was supported by training sessions for professionals such as probation officers and social workers, the results have been limited.

At much the same time in the US, Bob Custer in particular was involved in similar developments (Glen, Custer & Burns 1975; Custer & Custer 1978). Although the treatment approach advocated by Custer has been in operation for several years in a limited number of psychiatric centres there are no published data on the effectiveness, or otherwise, of this method of helping compulsive gamblers. Despite this the face validity of the treatment seems good and it is described in some detail below. The underlying philosophy of treatment reflects the same change that occurred in the UK – from treating the 'illness' to a problem-oriented approach. 'Treatment is directed toward the areas in which the pathological gambling has produced problems' (Custer 1982). The gambling itself is managed via referral to GA, with the explicit assumption that abstinence is the objective. The other basic goals of treatment are stated as 'full restitution' and 'assistance in developing constructive substitutes for gambling'. Although full restitution is a goal expressed by some compulsive gamblers, its inclusion in a description of a psychiatric treatment programme is intriguing and is discussed more fully later in this chapter. Admission to a psychiatric hospital is recommended where there is risk of suicide or where the gambler seems exhausted, isolated from family support or showing signs of emotional compensation. Initial assessment interviews provide information of the likely problems associated with the gambling:

1 Marital problems.
2 Immense debts.
3 Demands (and sometimes threats) from creditors.
4 Loss of employment.
5 Isolation from friends and relatives.
6 Legal problems.

The steps in treatment are:

1 To assist the patient to plan a rational approach to the solution of his problems (repayment plans consultation with a lawyer).
2 Rehabilitation to work, full employment as 'a substitute for their drive to gamble'.
3 Marital therapy.
4 Group therapy with other compulsive gamblers.

These, then, are the main recommendations for helping a compulsive gambler. At this stage one can only guess that if they were carried out by professional staff with experience of working with such patients they might well be effective for a good proportion of clients.

Certainly it is fair to say that in both the US and UK the psychiatric treatment of compulsive gamblers has come a long way from the use of LSD and referrals for psychoanalysis. Many fewer assumptions are now held by psychiatrists regarding the gambler; he or she is perceived more in terms of a person, often in acute distress, for whom a broad-based approach to assessment will provide a sound basis for planning help and treatment. Furthermore the gambler is considered not as an isolated 'sick person', but in the context of his or her interpersonal and social relationships. Moskowitz (1980) is an exception to this trend. He reported the treatment of three gamblers who were prescribed lithium carbonate on the basis that it might remove the 'thrill response' experienced by compulsive gamblers.

On both sides of the Atlantic the expertise and help available from GA is recognised and the use of their meetings in helping compulsive gamblers is explicitly recommended. Continued attendance at such meetings may provide long-term support in remaining abstinent from gambling. The main difference is that the US programmes are linked to a psychiatric centre with the compulsive gambler often being admitted to hospital. It is well established that such admissions often result in a variety of negative effects or personal costs to the individual (Trute & Loewen 1978). However, the UK attempt to shift the point of delivery of help away from psychiatric hospitals is not without its attendant shortcomings. The limited work done to date may have resulted in many social workers, probation officers, etc. being better prepared to help compulsive gamblers, but whether or not they have access to the range of resources such as financial and legal advice, marital therapy and so on, is another matter. The fact remains that compulsive gamblers are likely to continue to appear for treatment in psychiatric centres. To the psychiatrists involved, whether or not they have encountered previous 'Peters' or not it seems reasonable to commend the treatment programme described by Custer (1982).

Behaviour therapy

In this area of treatment research the reviewer is immediately struck by the fact that only two single case studies (Cotler 1971 and Bannister 1977) have been completed in the United States. This seems even more difficult to understand given the interest in behaviour therapy approaches expressed in a theoretical paper by Montgomery and Kreitzer in 1968. The use of aversion therapy in the United Kingdom will first be reviewed.

Although initially there appeared a number of reports in the literature (Barker & Miller 1966a, 1966b and 1968; Seager, Pokorny & Black 1966; Goorney 1968) the total number of cases was five; two poker-machine players and three who bet off-course on dogs and horses. In essence all were punished with painful electric shock while looking at stimuli associated with gambling, such as film of themselves placing a bet in a betting office. Prior to treatment, one poker-machine player commonly lost all his week's earnings in a single three- to four-hour session (Barker & Miller 1966a). Treatment consisted of four similar marathon sessions on a poker-machine that had been installed on the hospital premises. Electric shocks were delivered at random throughout these sessions at an average rate of almost one shock per minute, 672 shocks in total (shocks were reported to result in pronounced retraction of the forearm). At one year follow-up this man was no longer gambling but was given a 'booster' session following relapse and was then abstinent for another year. A similar approach with the other poker-machine player was unsuccessful. Abstinence was the outcome reported by the same authors (Barker & Miller 1968) for the gambler whose preference had been to bet in betting offices on horse and dog races. In this case electric shocks were delivered while the gambler viewed a film of himself betting. Interspersed were 'relief' stimuli – pictures of spouse and family – during which time no shocks were given. The case study by Goorney (1968) was very similar except that the gambler's selection of bets for the day's racing was also made the focus for a punishment procedure.

Seager (1970) reported using aversion therapy with sixteen gamblers. The gamblers were all men and all but one were off-course betters. The other was a roulette player. For the betting shop gamblers Seager summarised the betting sequence as follows:

1　Returns having lost any cash he may have had or borrowed.
2　Remorse. Promises wife that he will stop betting.
3　Selection of 'sure' bets from the morning paper.
4　Attempts to obtain money (unless payday).
5　Betting in shop until money gone or races over.

Although the theoretical basis of the treatment method was not discussed it seemed that the main objective was to disrupt the cyclical nature of the above sequence. Most of the gamblers had sessions that consisted of reading through a pile of assorted newspaper sheets in which were included racing pages at random intervals (on average 1 sheet in 4 contained information on the day's racing; meetings, runners, riders, form, etc.). Electric shocks were delivered to the gambler's left forearm ('sufficiently uncomfortable to cause definite discomfort, but no skin damage'), the shock continuing until the racing page was discarded. The gamblers who reported using the form guides in betting shops were shocked at random while viewing pictures of the interior of betting offices.

The overall plan of these treatment sessions was not stated and the number of sessions (of those who completed treatment) ranged from three to forty-two, yet the former received fifty shocks per session and the latter less than two! Although Seager stated that he thought treatment would be more effective if the gamblers were admitted to hospital, this proved impractical. Most gamblers felt that further time off work was unacceptable and only four unemployed gamblers were treated on an inpatient basis. Supportive psychotherapy and introduction to GA was offered after completion of the aversion therapy sessions.

The outcome of this work was that two gamblers refused to enter treatment when the procedure was explained to them and four more discontinued treatment after four or fewer sessions. Of the remaining ten, five were reported as definitely not gambling after twelve months or longer. (Three were reported to be in prison.)

Koller (1972), using a method similar to that of Barker and Miller (1968), treated twenty poker-machine addicts. Outcome data was reported for twelve of these with the time of follow-up ranging from two to five years. Six were abstinent and four gambling at a reduced level.

These, then, represent the reported studies using aversion therapy with gamblers. They have a similar ring to the early studies using the same procedures in relation to homosexuality, sexual deviance and alcoholism (for a review of this work see Rachman & Teasdale 1969). Although Peck (1973) reported that Seager had developed the apparently sophisticated anticipatory avoidance procedure of Feldman and MacCulloch (1971) for use with gamblers, there have been no results published to date.

From a theoretical standpoint the aversive method selected, generally a simple punishment procedure with the associated component of classical conditioning (i.e. the temporal association of gambling stimuli with electric shock) has been considered to be the most effective (Rachman & Teasdale 1969). In addition Seager's 'morning paper' session may be considered to satisfy several of the variables associated with the effectiveness of punishment procedures (Rimm & Masters 1979):

1 Immediacy of punishment – gamblers were shocked the moment they turned to the racing page.
2 Scheduling of punishment – gamblers were shocked every time they turned to the racing page.

3   Availability of alternative behaviours – gamblers could discard the racing page.

From an ethical standpoint there are two questions. The first concerns the use of *any* aversive procedure, and the second the manner in which the gamblers were introduced to the treatment. These are not separate issues. 'Aversion therapy should only be offered if other treatment methods are inapplicable and if the patient gives his permission after a consideration of all the information his therapist can honestly supply' (Rachman & Teasdale 1969: 174). Similar statements are now incorporated in codes of ethics generally shared by behaviour therapists (e.g. see the Association for Advancement of Behaviour Therapy statement on ethical issues in *Behaviour Therapy* **8**: v–vi).

Seager informed patients about the treatment he was proposing to use and indeed reminded the gamblers during treatment that they had the right to discontinue at any time. However, from a contemporary vantage-point it is difficult to understand why aversive methods were chosen at all. Given the plethora of personal, social and legal problems associated with the gamblers who were seeking help, why on earth sit them in a room and give shocks while they read the morning papers?

This is not intended as a self-righteous or easy condemnation of the work reviewed above. At that earlier time, the present author could similarly have been the focus of such criticism. Drawing on that experience, various factors can be identified that help explain why aversive methods were applied to gamblers. It is fair to say that given a 'new' problem, i.e. gamblers seeking help to control their betting, the range of treatment options was limited. The term 'treatment' itself is a helpful reminder that all the work reported above was completed in a hospital setting with its attendant procedures, language and isolation, certainly from the realities of betting shops and casinos. (A straw count of psychiatrists and psychologists over the years suggests that only one in fifty may ever have visited a betting office.)

Today, the acceptance of the multi-causality of behaviour has been associated with the development of an impressive range of multi-component social learning programmes, especially in the very areas where aversive methods were originally employed, such as sexual deviance and the addictive behaviours. For this reason alone there are no ground for recommending that compulsive gamblers should be offered a limited technique such as aversion therapy. The reports reviewed above provide no evidence to suggest that aversive techniques when used with gamblers were any more effective than psychoanalysis, group therapy or, one is tempted to add, a placebo, or even doing nothing at all.

The remainder of the behaviour therapy literature in this area illustrates the vagaries of interest in compulsive gamblers and may be said at times to be entertaining rather than informative. For example, Peck and Ashcroft (1972) reported using 'stimulus satiation' with five gamblers. The concept has been variously defined and was used in the treatment of a mental hospital patient who hoarded towels – she was given them eventually at the rate of sixty per day until the habit was extinguished (Ayllon 1963) – and more recently in modifying smoking behaviour (Best Owen & Trentadue 1978). In the case of gamblers the theroretical assumption was that the cues associated with gambling behaviour generated a drive; perhaps in a similar manner to that proposed by McConaghy (1980) for the behaviour completion mechanism. Repeated exposure to such cues, it was hypothesised, would lead to a reduction in the drive to gamble and in the behaviour itself.

In order to achieve this the authors described a procedure whereby the gambler was admitted to hospital, his room was decorated with racing posters, form, runners and riders, race commentaries were played through loudspeakers, two daily racing papers were delivered each morning and staff were instructed to talk with the patient only about gambling. Escape from this environment was only permitted to the toilet, where presumably there were yet more racing magazines. The outcome of this procedure was somewhat loosely specified: 'For four out of the five patients gambling ceased to be a major problem.' The authors noted that the procedure might allow of alternative explanations such as aversion or extinction but commended its use, as it 'makes comparatively little demand on the therapist's time'! As discussed earlier, Peck and Ashcroft's (1972) report underlined the important theoretical and research question regarding the triggering effect of cues specific to gambling. As a treatment approach its use parallels recent conclusions regarding satiation procedures in smoking research: 'It (satiation) may be a very useful element of a multicomponent treatment' (Pechacek & Danaher 1979).

The remaining published reports on the behavioural treatment of gamblers are three single-case studies: Cotler (1971), Bannister (1977) and Dickerson and Weeks (1979). Cotler's was the first published attempt to alter reinforcement contingencies, not just in a hospital environment but in the gambler's own life situation. The approach was based on the theoretical suggestions of Montgomery and Kreitzer (1968), namely that the treatment programme should focus on certain 'intervention points':

1 The gambler choosing not to gamble when opportunity occurs.
2 Choosing to stop when losing.
3 Involvement in non-gambling activities.

Treatment reflected this complexity, as aversive techniques, massed practice and time out (from spouse) were all used to eliminate gambling behaviour, along with positive reinforcement and agreeing with other members of the family to increase the frequency of 'more desirable and appropriate behaviours'. Following a booster treatment after a return to betting at nine months, the result at two years was cessation of gambling. Cotler emphasised the importance of a one to two year follow-up as an integral part of treatment. Although only a single case this report showed a theoretical depth and consistency, with the procedures adopted all having the objective of enabling the gambler to retain control of, or cope effectively with, gambling cues and betting behaviour itself. These themes show good 'fit' with the more recently defined concept of self-efficacy (Bandura 1977). Gathercole (1973), in a speculative paper, explored a very similar treatment approach by considering the ways in which a residential hostel for compulsive gamblers might adopt a programme of management along token economy lines, reinforcing reductions in gambling behaviour and the development of alternative patterns of behaviour.

Bannister (1977) represents the only purely cognitive approach to treating a compulsive gambler. Using rational emotive therapy and covert sensitisation the outcome at one year was successful elimination of gambling. Dickerson and Weeks (1979) broke no new ground regarding therapeutic techniques. The pragmatic use of explicit cash control as a basis for agreement between the marital partners permitted the gambler to maintain a much reduced and controlled level of betting. The main objective of the report was to draw attention to parallels with research in alcoholism by documenting the ability of a compulsive gambler to maintain, at least at fifteen months follow-up, a controlled level of betting.

Throughout the above behaviour therapy literature there are no reports of any controlled treatment trials that in any way approach acceptable standards of evaluation (see, for example, Kazdin & Wilson 1978). It is not known which behavioural techniques work (permit a gambler to stop or regain control of his or her betting). There is, however, a trend away from the use of single limited procedures such as aversion therapy toward a multimodal approach.

Gamblers Anonymous

Friday the 13th would seem the appropriate day on which

to found a gamblers' self-help group. This marked the beginning of Gamblers Anonymous (GA) in September 1957 in Los Angeles, California. In the subsequent twenty-five years the organisation, together with its sister group, Gam Anon (for spouses and families of compulsive gamblers), has grown to be a world-wide organisation with almost 500 chapters (groups that meet weekly). Gamblers Anonymous is well established in Australia, New Zealand, the United Kingdom and, of course, the United States.

The group describes itself as a spiritual movement and in its 'Unity Programme' states that each chapter or group should be self-governing, the organisation as a whole to be apolitical, self-financing, avoiding publicity and with the minimum number of members involved in maintaining the organisation at local and national level. The only requirement for GA membership is an expressed desire to stop gambling. As the GA philosophy and group method are based very closely upon that of Alcoholics Anonymous it is not surprising that GA literature and the members themselves adopt a disease explanation of compulsive gambling:

> What is the first thing a compulsive gambler ought to do in order to stop gambling? He must accept the fact that he is in the grip of a progressive illness and have the desire to get well . . . The first small bet to a problem gambler is like the first small drink to an alcoholic. Sooner or later he falls back into the same old destructive pattern. (From GA pamphlet *Questions and Answers About the Problem of Compulsive Gambling* and the GA Recovery Programme.)

Thus, abstinence from gambling, and indeed avoidance of all forms of betting including lotteries, raffles and pools, is the prescribed goal. A knowledge of the possible causal factors resulting in a person becoming a compulsive gambler are not considered important to recovery but are nonetheless listed as:

1 Inability and unwillingness to accept reality; the gambler escapes into a dream world.
2 Emotional insecurity; a sense of acceptance only experienced when gambling.
3 Immaturity; desire to be powerful, to have all the good things effortlessly.

Success through the Recovery Programme is considered to come about by the gambler slowly changing his own personality. 'To recover from one of the most baffling, insidious, compulsive addictions will require diligent effort. Honesty, open mindedness, willingness are the keywords in our recovery.' One final concept concerns the importance of spiritual aspects. Will power or self-control are considered to be important but not to be relied upon, 'but adherence to spiritual principles seems to solve our problems. Most of us feel that a belief in a Power greater than ourselves is necessary in order to sustain a desire to refrain from gambling.' The religious and moral overtones present in the written materials are in this author's experience invariably found in the group meetings themselves. This may, however, have been different in the early days of the organisation in the United States when Scodel (1964) considered that GA was exhortative and caused the formation of an isolated deviant group.

At a practical level GA consists of weekly meetings of a group of gamblers that may number anything from two to twenty members. The routine followed varies from group to group and country to country but roughly consists of:

1 All members in turn state 'My name is _____, I'm a compulsive gambler and I have/have not gambled this week (had a bust; had a fall).'
2 Those new to the group and those reporting a bust are questioned and advised by other group members.
3 Members in turn read from the Unity Programme and the Recovery Programme.
4 'Therapies', (5–10 minute personal memories about gambling) are given by selected members. These are

formally applauded to acknowledge that the person has contributed to the group and told the truth.

This may take an hour or more and is followed by coffee and informal talking in twos and threes.

Much detailed advice is offered when gamblers describe some recent return to gambling or a related problem. When a new member attends he or she will often have had some personal contact with an established GA member. Thus there is initially some individual counselling and this may continue as a supportive relationship in addition to the group work. Advice is essentially practical, focusing on:

1 An initial budget.
2 Setting low regular repayment of debts (to ensure that the gambler is not additionally stressed and encouraged to return to gambling).
3 Controlling access to cash.
4 Organising work schedules that prevent access to gambling environments.
5 Negotiating with spouse and developing trust between marital partners.

At times of stress or when a member feels they are about to have a bust, he or she is encouraged to phone any other member and talk.

Gam Anon meetings are usually concurrent but separate and are mainly attended by the spouses of gamblers who are members of GA. The aims and methods are less clearly defined but 'are all designed to teach the family of the compulsive gambler to understand him and to live with or without him'. Margaret (aged 25) provides a commonly occurring example of the work done in the Gam Anon group. After attending for several weeks and responding with relief to the stories in common with other wives she reported in tears her husband's recent bust, his first in three weeks. It transpired that she had gone away for the weekend with their two young children to stay at the coast; before leaving she had given her husband two envelopes, one containing cash to pay the rent and the other for their newly opened savings account. On her return she found out that her husband had been back on the poker machines and had lost both amounts of money and some of his wages too before he had been able to stop. By the end of the meeting she realised that her husband's 'illness' was a long-term problem and that she had to play her part by planning day-by-day and sticking to their agreed system of controlling the cash. Where the spouse or family attend Gam Anon and report that the gambler does not want to stop or attend GA the support and advice is geared toward helping the development of independence. Some problems recur and preclude easy solutions, in particular when a spouse is faced with the choice of providing cash or letting their gambler partner go to court and possibly to gaol.

Gamblers Anonymous collects no evaluative data. Their success rate is not known. It has been estimated that two in every five first-time attenders continue, to become regulars and hence to remain abstinent with some busts (Dickerson 1974). Brown (1973) reported on a comparison of lapsed members with regular pinholders (pins or badges indicate the number of years without a bet). Difficulties in obtaining a response from and even locating the lapsed members (those who attended at least once resulted in interviews with about 10 per cent of the total. The tentative conclusions were that lapsed members reacted with elation and felt 'cured' at the first meeting; they saw themselves as having mild problems compared with other members. Continued attendance was associated with having very large debts or none at all. Those who lapsed were more likely to have debts amounting to two to three months' income. The handbook was highly valued by lapsed and regular members. Based on his enquiry and on his own lengthy experience of working with GA, Brown concluded that GA was in some respects a successful organisation, having an impact especially on those who returned for a second meeting but also on those who attended only once. An impact on the latter was in terms of their recall of this one opportunity to meet other compulsive gamblers, their belief that they would return at some future time and finally their continued use of the handbook. Brown also listed three aspects of GA groups that might contribute to non-attendance:

1   Domination of the group by an inner clique.
2   Busts or falls reacted to by primitive attitudes and emotions before the facts of the event have been clarified.
3   A tendency to assume that membership requires very heavy gambling and massive problems.

It is difficult to generalise these findings to any other GA group and one can only speculate about the likely efficacy of the organisation in terms of the help it provides to individual gamblers. It is reliably documented (Custer & Custer 1978) that some gamblers may succeed in stopping gambling by attending GA meetings and applying the Recovery Programme to their day-to-day living, without having any additional help. The 'best guess' of the rate of success is 40 per cent of first-time attenders.

Some aspects of GA philosophy may detract from its effectiveness. The belief that compulsive gambling is an illness is a key concept and asserted at every meeting. This rigidity may lead to the exclusion of those who experience loss of control of their gambling behaviour and want help but reject the idea that they are ill. On the other hand the use of the illness concept may initially be of great relief to the spouse or family, alleviating guilt and shame and providing a way of understanding the problem. Abstinence may also be a barrier to some new members, particularly when rigidly applied even to raffles, draws and football pools. Not all groups reject all forms of gambling and similarly groups may have different attitudes to advertising their existence. This latter point seems to be the most obvious way in which GA fails to take full advantage of its unique expertise in helping gamblers. In many groups even the use of a small-ad in a local paper is vetoed.

Recent developments, especially in the US have

resulted in a much closer and planned cooperation between professional workers in treatment centres and local GA stalwarts. Some of these members receive a training so that they may more effectively combine their own personal experience of gambling with counselling skills. From the professionals standpoint, whether working to psychiatric facilities, social work or probation services, an involvement with such a voluntary organisation can be a very effective use of resources. Gamblers Anonymous can be viewed as a small part of an increasing network of self-help groups that provides support for a range of addictive types of problems such as alcohol abuse, smoking, drugs and compulsive eating. The involvement of psychologists and other professionals in such networks seems a viable alternative to working in a traditional manner in hospitals and health centres (Sarason *et al.* 1977; McPherson & Sutton 1981). For GA itself the obvious payoffs are to enhance the help they give and to evaluate routinely their success.

There is a need for the group method to be used more flexibly, perhaps developing methods of providing individual counselling for new members together with their spouses; 'therapies' in group meetings need to be relatively short and to draw upon recent experience and memories, not the repetition of life histories. Some attempt should be made to record the range of techniques successfully used to control cash and predictive information about the times when falls or busts are more likely to occur. These apparent 'mere details' are in fact the way in which the Recovery Programme is implemented and tailored to fit the individual's needs. It is a rich vein of practical solutions to the problem of regaining self-control.

In the US the establishment of the National Council on Compulsive Gambling has played a part in aiding the development of GA and providing public recognition of the work it has done over a quarter of a century. Often this work has been carried out without any parallel support or help from professional helping agencies. Even today among professionals knowledge and experience of helping compulsive gamblers is scant. Despite their conceptual and methodological inadequacies, Gamblers Anonymous remain the experts in the field of helping compulsive gamblers.

Contemporary developments in the provision of help

In the United States, House Bill 1311 was enacted in the 1978 session of the Maryland General Assembly. It stated (from Politzer and Morrow 1980):

1   that compulsive gambling is a serious social problem and there is evidence that availability of gambling increases the risk of becoming a compulsive gambler, and

2   that Maryland with its extensive legalised gambling has an obligation to provide treatment for those persons who become addicted to gambling to the extent that it seriously disrupts lives and families.'

The Bill directed that a pilot project centre be established for the provision of treatment for compulsive gamblers and their families. When, in 1979, this law became effective, six other states were introducing or preparing similar legislation. At a congressional level there were moves to establish a National Commission on Compulsive Gambling with the objective of assessing the dimensions of the problem.

The Maryland legislation represents the first time that any society has accepted that by permitting and deriving revenue from legalised gambling, it had a social responsibility to provide help for those who became addicted. The 'help' took the form of the Compulsive Gambling Counselling Center under the aegis of Johns Hopkins University. Although the origins of this Center are unique, it was the fourth such treatment programme for compulsive gamblers to be established in the United States. The previous three had all been Veterans Administration initiatives (Cleveland in 1972; Brooklyn and Miami in 1977). All were hospital-based programmes using in- and out-patient facilities. All three, and the Johns Hopkins' Center, show great similarities, probably reflecting Bob Custer's influential role in their establishment. The kind of treatment provided has already been outlined in the section on psychiatric treatment. Here it will suffice to review briefly the themes common to all the programmes and finally to emphasise two important additional aspects of the Johns Hopkins' Center.

Themes in common are:

1   *Restitution.* In the treatment of compulsive gamblers it is assumed that the repayment of all debts is a desirable goal. This assumption, and the reasons for it have not yet been discussed. It may be that the goal of repaying debts is espoused by all gamblers who seek help. It may be that in many cases the institution of regular, albeit small, repayments is the only way of avoiding a prison sentence. Perhaps repayment may play an important part in restoring self-esteem and alleviating guilt and shame. In some instances the duration of repayments may stretch dauntingly years ahead and be a counterproductive aspect of treatment. Restitution as an integral part of treatment requires analysis and empirical evaluation, if only to ensure that the psychologists and psychiatrists involved are not merely expressing their own value system.

2   *Here-and-now problem-solving approach.* Although research at Miami (Moravec 1980) is oriented toward aetiology in that extensive psychological assessment is used to evaluate types of personality prone to become addicted to gambling, all centres focues upon crisis resolution, budgeting, employment, etc.

3   *Involvement with Gamblers Anonymous.* This is an integral part of all programmes. Compulsive gamblers are introduced or reintroduced to GA.

4   The use of group therapy and the frequent involvement of families.

5   Assistance in the resolution of legal problems.
6   The use of both inpatient and outpatient facilities. Although the admission of compulsive gamblers occurs, as one would expect, more regularly in the hospital-based programmes, even Johns Hopkins' Center has the use of two beds for use by out-of-state referrals. As stated earlier, Custer (1982) elaborated various admission criteria, notably for those persons where suicide was deemed likely.

These, then, are the main similarities, and although the programmes have their different emphases – vocational evaluation in Brooklyn and psychological testing in Miami – two features of the Johns Hopkins' Center merit comment. First, instead of using doctoral-level psychologists as the main therapists the emphasis is on peer counselling by trained GA members together with counsellors from a range of health and mental health professions. Second, programme evaluation has been integrated into all levels of service delivery. One of the main instruments used to assess the quality of care is the Goal Attainment Scale which permits the 'success' of clients to be assessed individually. Preliminary outcome data indicated that the frequency of gambling was lowered in 100 per cent of cases, restitution was attained as planned or better by 67 per cent, improved family relationships were attained by 75 per cent and improvement in self-esteem was attained 'as expected' in over 80 per cent of cases.

In Australia a major treatment programme is nearing completion, the first stage of which was described by McConaghy *et al.* (1982). When completed, the total number of compulsive gamblers treated will be eighty. The origins of the project are to be found in the theoretical hypothesis that behaviour completion mechanisms maintain compulsive behavioural patterns (McConaghy 1980) and the research design reflects this theoretical interest.

A planned sequence of four paired treatment comparisons has been completed but follow-up data are not yet available for the latter parts of the programme (Blaszczynski 1982). The treatment comparisons included aversive-relief versus desensitisation and relaxation versus desensitisation. Gamblers seeking help to reduce their urge to gamble were recruited to the programme provided they were not overtly psychotic. In the first stage of the programme seventeen men and thee women were treated during a one-week admission to a psychiatric unit. Those receiving the aversive-relief treatment read aloud from a sequence of cards a brief description of a gambling situation and at the same time imagined themselves in that situation. Immediately the gambler finished reading the card an unpleasant electric shock was delivered to the non-dominant hand. After every sequence of ten or so cards a relief card describing some behaviour incompatible with gambling, e.g. playing at home with the children, was included and not followed by shock. Fourteen treatment sessions were given during the week and in all approximately 500 shocks were experienced by each gambler. Desensitisation consisted of brief relaxation training followed by fourteen treatment sessions in which the gambler, while relaxed, imagined entering a gambling situation and avoiding gambling, for example by leaving and returning home. Each imaginal sequence was presented step by step with the gambler signalling when he was relaxed after each step.

Pre-treatment, one month and one year post-treatment assessments were completed by an independent assessor blind to the nature of the treatment received. At one year the desensitisation procedure was significantly more effective in reducing both the urge to gamble and gambling behaviour itself. Desensitisation was also associated with a significant reduction in anxiety (measured by Spielberger's State-Trait Anxiety Inventory; Spielberger, Gorsuch & Lushene 1970).

Conclusions

There exists at present no one established means of helping people to stop or regain control of their gambling behaviour. However, from the evidence it can be concluded that there are no grounds for recommending psychoanalysis or aversion therapy. The trend toward an individually tailored problem-oriented approach has face validity but there is a lack of evaluative information. As a cautionary note it may help once again to draw a parallel with the research findings in alcoholism where the effectiveness of 'total push' residential treatment programmes, used as the model for the hospital-based gambling programmes in the United States, may be no better than a single one-hour consultation providing information and giving advice (Edwards *et al.* 1977).

Two themes, the development of closer collaboration between health-care professionals and Gamblers Anonymous and the attempts in the UK to move the point of delivery of help away from psychiatric centres, merit further consideration.

Of the recent developments the Johns Hopkins' project appears to be a model for applied evaluative research. In contrast, the work in Australia with its emphasis on limited procedures appears dated. Despite this and the weaknesses inherent in the theoretical model, the programme's sound methodology may permit the evaluation of specific techniques for inclusion in future multifaceted approaches to helping gamblers.

Chapter 7

How to stop or regain control: a practical guide

The following is an expanded version of the *Guide* (Dickerson 1975) published by the UK Consultation on 'Compulsive' Gambling. Its original objective was to encourage agencies to offer help directly to men and women with gambling problems rather than to believe that a referral to a specialist was required. Here additional information has been added so that it can be used by gamblers in a self-help fashion.

The following assumptions have been made:

1 The helper and/or the gambler has checked out all those aspects of living that may be adversely affected by regular gambling – marital, economic, employment and legal – and has where necessary sought specialist help from a marital counsellor, lawyer, etc.

2 There is no one established form of management for gambling problems.

3 The gambler has at least one person (a counsellor, spouse, friend) with whom they have made a definite agreement to work on the problem.

4 Where a chapter of GA is available the gambler will consider attendance as his or her best means of obtaining continued long-term support.

5 Most gamblers who seek help admit lying about their gambling, even when they do not need to, and this habit does not disappear merely because they have

sought help. Both helper and gambler should realise that this may be a problem, especially when starting work together. Sometimes it may be helpful to deal with the topic quite openly: talking about some of the 'worst' lies told in the past, discussing how inaccurate information may undermine the work on the problem; noting the times in the future when being honest may be difficult and planning ways of overcoming this – by developing an accurate diary of events, giving news of a bust over the phone before meeting face to face, etc.

6 Both gambler and helper agree that the helper has no part in providing cash or obtaining access to loans, etc.

The practical guide below is concerned solely with the aim of helping to regain control of expenditure on gambling, whether the preference is to stop gambling altogether or to limit spending to a predetermined level.

There are three main themes;

1 Control of cash flow.
2 Increasing alternative activities incompatible with uncontrolled gambling.
3 Long-term considerations.

Control of cash flow

1 Establish the full extent and nature of debts: this is commonly the most difficult area for completely open communication and the helper should not be surprised if 'new' debts are discovered.
2 Establish priorities for all outgoings including preferred level of spending on gambling and write an explicit budget. If this includes debt repayment start with small regular amounts, as pressure for money increases the likelihood of further loss of control of gambling.
3 Make plans for controlling the flow of cash. This depends on the extent of the gambler's experience of loss of control. Some people (perhaps 20%) give up

gambling quite easily, and at the other extreme some gamblers believe they are quite unable to have cash in their hands without gambling. Where there are problems of self-control there is a range of cash flow controls that can be established and varied according to the needs of the individual and as progress is made.

(a) Inform the family and extended family and friends of the plans that have been made and that lending money can lead to further problems.

(b) Arrange for wages to be paid directly into a bank, savings account or collected by a marital partner.

(c) Arrange to have accounts operated by two signatures, or not at all by the gambler.

(d) Whenever possible pay major outgoings by banker's order or cheques and avoid having sums of cash around the house.

(e) When social outings require cash, take only a planned amount, e.g. enough for a couple of rounds of drinks.

(f) Where there is no one in the gambler's life to share the organisation of cash control the helper may be prepared to take a direct role in the matter; in addition, some banks may accept an arrangement whereby wages are transferred to a 'closed' account which, by standing order, feeds small sums every two or three days to a current account, access to which is only possible via a bank machine, thus preventing overdrawing and bouncing cheques.

4 Make all cash flow 'visible'. Where the gambler is in a marriage or similar relationship, trust can be built up by the use of bank statements and receipts to support agreements. Keeping a small sum of cash available in public (e.g. in a pot on a shelf) for use for petrol, cigarettes, beer or coffee can provide the gambler with opportunities to handle cash without risking large sums of money.

5 Anticipate changes in life style, such as holidays,

changing· jobs, and moving house, and plan any additional cash-flow controls.

6   When control of gambling expenditure is the aim, keep written accounts of all stakes, losses and winnings.

Increasing alternative activities incompatible with uncontrolled gambling

As some regular gamblers spend, for example, thirty hours a week gambling, stopping or cutting back may leave a void. Self-control can be aided by carefully planning each day so that work and other commitments are arranged to conflict with the opportunity to bet.

1   Appointments may be deliberately planned to clash with times most usually spent gambling, e.g. the beginning of racing. When this is not possible and/or gambling is associated with the type of job or with workmates, control may be achieved only by changing to a job which makes rigid demands upon time and prevents access to gambling.

2   Change the expectancies of friends and workmates by giving them information about the problem and the plans made to deal with it; this is hard to do at first but can lead to useful support when most needed.

3   An additional job may help and may also assist in resolving cash shortages.

4   Sometimes the gambler may wish to have greater involvement with his/her spouse and family.

5   Social and personal interests such as hobbies and sport may be developed.

   When the objective is to continue gambling in a controlled manner, limiting and providing outside checks on the cash and time available can be made more effective by altering aspects of the gambling behaviour itself, as follows:

6   Try stopping gambling completely for two weeks; this can help the gambler estimate how much control can

be exerted simply by deciding to stop for an agreed time.

7   For off-course betting, select and write out bets away from the bookies and place bets only outside the hours of racing or well before the bet-on event takes place.

8   For gambling that involves a skill component emphasise this aspect – get access to detailed form guides, use betting accounting systems to see whether winnings rise as skill improves.

9   For gambling such as roulette and poker machines try several consecutive visits to the club with a helping friend, without playing. If physical tension, sweating, tremor, and so on, is experienced then stay for at least an hour or until these feelings have decreased. Repeat these visits without playing until these feelings are experienced only slightly or not at all.

10 Choosing to gamble in places where continuous play is possible requires predetermining the amount of cash to be taken. In some club and casino settings it may be difficult for regular good customers to maintain limits on cash spending as various cheque or credit facilities may be made available.

11 Challenge any irrational patterns of thinking and beliefs held about gambling, especially where chance games are seen as skillful. Examples are the use of systems in roulette as a means of winning and beliefs that a poker machine is about to give a jackpot. On index cards write out rational statements such as:

'Last year I lost 2,500 pounds/dollars.'
'Regularly switching my bet at the last minute means I'm behind and losing my nerve.'
'After a run of losers raising my stakes and betting on outsiders is dumb.'
'If I regularly play the poker machines, in the long run I cannot win; I will lose on average 15 per cent of my stake.'

'For every spin in roulette on average I will lose $2\frac{1}{2}$ per cent of my stake.'

Reading these cards regularly can help establish rational patterns of thinking that may help control expenditure on gambling.

12 When uncontrolled gambling seems to be regularly triggered off by reading the sports page, after going to a particular bar with racing on TV, working in a part of town near a bookie or a club, then try avoiding these. Obviously it is not possible to avoid all contact with gambling news and information but when trying to re-establish control even something like stopping buying/reading a morning paper can help.

Long-term considerations

It is often easy to change all sorts of addictive types of behaviour such as smoking, excessive drinking and over-eating in the short term, but much more difficult to sustain these changes over a period of two or more years. This is certainly true of gambling and there is a variety of ways of tackling this aspect of the problem.

1 Ensure ongoing help or support for at least two years even if meetings become infrequent when things are going well; attendance at GA meetings can help maintain motivation to keep working on the problem.

2 Make the successful control of cash rewarding, e.g. celebrating debt repayment. Re-establish associations between money and non-gambling activities – buying clothes, sports equipment, household items, taking a holiday, taking out health/life assurance, donating to charities or churches, joining a political party.

3 Expect returns to loss of control to occur and learn to predict times when this is most likely and explore coping strategies. Most busts or falls occur after periods of feeling frustrated, angry or depressed and such feelings can serve as an early-warning system and lead to

phoning a friend or GA member, arranging some vigorous sporting activity or reintroducing tight cash controls as a safeguard.

4 When losing control of gambling happens, use it as an event from which to learn; what were the strengths and weaknesses of the coping strategies? Remember that the urge to bet may reappear without any apparent reason for a short while even after a year or more of control or abstinence.

5 Review progress and plans at least twice a year, even when things are going well. In particular explore whether controls on cash may be slowly relaxed to permit greater independence. Some gamblers prefer not to have access to large cash sums for many years, others seem not to find it a problem.

Chapter 8

Conclusions

Causes of high-frequency gambling

Despite the lack of a consistent theme or direction to research into habitual gambling there is now available a wealth of detail regarding such behaviour, although much of the work requires further validation and development. The assumptions that gamblers who seek help are mentally disordered or have a personality that predisposes them to gamble heavily have not been substantiated. Such conclusions have been drawn too readily on the basis of the comparison of the characteristics of those who seek help with those of hypothetical social gamblers who bet infrequently. It seems that so-called 'compulsive' gamblers are not uniquely different from many other habitual gamblers who may neither want nor seek help to reduce or control their gambling.

There is evidence to suggest that high-frequency gamblers in roulette and in off-course betting (where a commentary is provided) develop patterns of betting behaviour that are different from low-frequency punters. Some habitual gamblers consistently place their stakes as late as possible in the cycle of events and may hold beliefs and theories that it is skilful to do so. In poker-machine play high-frequency gamblers may use several machines at once, believe that there is a skill component involved in their play, and be motivated by the goal of winning jackpots.

Maintaining control seems to be an important aspect of high-frequency gambling and people use various methods to achieve this, with more or less success. Some gamblers describe a powerful subjective urge to bet more, either during a session or when away from a gambling environment. This urge may be enhanced by a sequence of losing bets resulting in further betting with increased stakes and/or longer odds; 'chasing', as it is called. Loss of control has been defined in terms of spending more time and money than planned or losing all available cash-in-hand. Control is clearly not an all-or-none phenomenon but varies between individuals and within the same person from occasion to occasion. At transition points from lower to higher frequencies of gambling, cognitive factors, such as perceiving the game as skill-determined, may lead to persistence when losing and thereby contribute to difficulties in maintaining self-control.

Of all the concepts in psychology those pertaining to 'self' are among the most difficult to define and explore (Epstein 1980). However as the theme of self-control seems central to much of what has so far been established for high-frequency gamblers, some brief speculation may be justified. Self-control has some connotations of accord between behaviour and cognitions; not that people's actions invariably match their expressed intentions and preferences. Furthermore, the degree of accord will vary for different behaviours at different times. However, when behaviours consistently fail to match expressed intentions then this may be associated with a subjective feeling of discomfort both by the person concerned and those with whom he or she relates. Thus in a clinical setting a person with a compulsive cleaning ritual may be rational and accept that a particular object cannot harm them and yet, when at home, lose control and repeat the protective ritual. There is thus a discordance between the 'preferred' belief and actual behaviour. Generally speaking, most observers of gamblers who persist despite losing have assumed that such behaviour is irrational – that it illustrates discordance similar to the person completing a compulsive ritual. However Oldman's (1974, 1978) observations made the important point that this is not invariably the case. Some habitual gamblers may choose to lose money as a part of their leisure activity and in a financial and legal crisis a person may rationally risk losing even more money on the chance of winning sufficient to retrieve the situation. However, for most high-frequency gamblers their persistence when losing does illustrate discordance between beliefs and actions. At the extreme are persons who state they are losing and that they want to stop or reduce their betting yet cannot achieve this. Other gamblers may not be aware of the irrationality of their own behaviour if, for example, they believe that late betting is skilful or a means of beating the croupier. When skill is relevant to a form of gambling, as in horse- and dog-race betting, the discordance between belief and actions is harder to tease out. None the less there is evidence that as the frequency of betting increases so does the belief that one's selection involves more skill and yet the observed behaviour actually becomes less skilful, with escalating stakes, hurried bet selection and last-minute changes in selections.

It is difficult to assess the extent to which cognitions and beliefs maintain habitual gambling but at the very least they may serve to obscure the self-perception that one's gambling is out of control. This aspect of gambling requires more careful definition and evaluation. A better understanding of loss of control or craving has been a focus for recent reappraisal in other addictions such as alcoholism (Hodgson, Rankin and Stockwell 1979; Rankin, Hodgson & Stockwell 1979). In gambling, the determinants and subjective experiences of control may be more open to examination in the absence of any toxic effects of a psychoactive agent.

Another potentially heuristic concept in understanding

the addictions generally is that of learning. In gambling this may involve operant schedules of intermittent cash reinforcement and a classical conditioning component, whereby physiological changes are repeatedly associated with particular stimulus events such as the spinning of the roulette wheel and ball, revolving poker-machine reels and race commentaries. Whether during gambling this results in increased arousal (perceived as excitement) or in reductions, as in compulsive behaviours, is not known. It seems likely that the former may be more important but both changes may occur at different times within a session and from one session to another depending on the basal level of arousal and mood prior to gambling. Studies of autonomic arousal, subjective experiences and betting behaviours during sessions of gambling in real environments would provide data to evaluate such hypotheses.

The structural characteristics of gambling, particularly the duration of a sequence, its frequency per unit time and stake size, are probably important factors in persistence. Future research would benefit from the development of some measure of these and other characteristics, such as those defined by Weinstein and Deitch (1974), so that comparisons might be made more readily across different forms of gambling. Finally, there is a need for long-term research to address the question of the development of habitual gambling; the only data available at present are retrospective.

Developments in the provision of help for gamblers

Apart from GA and a very limited number of treatment programmes, there is little organised help for gamblers. Although some of the gambler's problems, such as personal isolation, marital breakdown, employment and legal difficulties will be similar to those of many other people seeking help from a variety of agencies, the gambling behaviour itself may require some unique form of intervention. At present it is not possible to conclude how best to achieve goals of abstinence or control. Research findings do permit the conclusion that expensive or unpleasant treatments, psychoanalysis and aversion therapy respectively, are no more effective than any other method. Current evaluative studies should help clarify the situation and assist in the development of techniques to facilitate control of gambling rather than abstinence. In addition the assumption that debts should be repayed in full merits research evaluation. When complete restitution involves many years of repayments this may represent a stress that contributes to relapse. Matching a gambler's debt repayments dollar for dollar with treatment funds might result in more effective intervention and be a further indication of the state's acceptance that such problems, relatively infrequent though they may be, are part and parcel of legalised gambling.

At present the availability of help for gamblers may be a more important consideration than the method of intervention. It makes good sense that any helping agency should feel competent to provide help to gamblers rather than assume that such people require referral to specialist psychiatric care. Where psychiatric centres have achieved a level of expertise in helping gamblers it seems important that they should develop networks within the surrounding community, including maintaining links with GA, so that help is more readily available outside the limitations of an institutional setting.

Social considerations

The development of coherent social policies in regard to high-frequency gambling is not possible in the absence of epidemiological data. The need for more detailed and reliable information about participation in gambling was stressed in the Rothschild Report (HMSO 1978). Future studies should also attempt to assess the related costs of habitual gambling, including marital breakdown, working days lost and criminal offences.

In alcoholism the frequency of parallel alcohol-related problems such as drink-and-driving offences and physical complications is closely related to the availability and cost of alcoholic drinks (Schmidt 1977; Harvard 1977). If similarities between alcoholism and high-frequency gambling continue to be justified, then the extent of the related personal and social costs of gambling will also be a function of its availability; the more gambling, the more people with related problems. Thus, to paraphrase Kendell (1979): 'Habitual gambling; a therapeutic or a political problem?' In the US the state-financed treatment programmes may be one kind of answer.

As far as political answers are concerned, if prohibition of gambling is seen as unpopular, ineffective and costly to police then behavioural science might usefully contribute to the selection of forms of gambling that provide the service most people want yet minimise the occurrence of related problems. One example concerns the design of off-course betting facilities. There is a variety of these currently in use in different countries. Data from behaviour analysis have suggested that repeated betting and listening to race commentaries may result in gamblers experiencing difficulty in maintaining control of the frequency of betting and the amount staked. Thus the design of the off-course betting office may influence the occurrence of gambling-related personal and social problems. The following rank-order of existing facilities might represent the ease with which the respective customers may control their betting (i.e. 1–4 below represents increasing difficulty in maintaining control).

1 In France the Paris-Mutuel Urbain premises provide a counter with room for one or two people and there is no betting during racing hours.
2 In New York there is plenty of space for people to meet and talk but no race commentary.
3 In Australia there is space, a race commentary but no form guides.
4 In the UK there is space, commentaries, form guides

and by law there is no open view in or out of the premises.

The above ordering of the different off-course facilities may parallel a customer's increasing difficulty in controlling his or her betting. Hence the UK betting office may be the most costly in terms of related personal and social problems.

The data required to evaluate such a hypothesis are not available and governments generally have not attempted routinely to collect information about participation in gambling. (Information in terms of average family expenditure is accepted to be misleading as expenditure on gambling is a highly skewed distribution with a small minority of gamblers generating a disproportionately large percentage of the total sums staked.) At present the research data suggest that it is only a small percentage of regular gamblers who encounter a crisis point involving a complex of personal problems. Although there may be several others indirectly affected, in no way does this represent a major threat to the social fabric of the countries in which various forms of gambling have been legalised. None the less the personal suffering of those directly and indirectly affected may be severe and it seems reasonable that facilities offering help should be made available.

That there has generally been a failure to provide such help is surprising and perhaps this may be a function of the moral overtones that tend to pervade the formulation of social policies concerning gambling. The way in which moral judgements have clouded important issues can be illustrated by comparison with attitudes and policies concerning another leisure activity, hang-gliding. As a fairly recent addition to the range of leisure activities, it seemed obvious and acceptable that certain controls and regulations should be introduced to safeguard the individual's use of this new piece of apparatus, the hang-glider itself. The development of the sport was monitored, training and contruction standards were developed and accidents recorded. In contrast, in the UK the Betting and Gaming

Act 1960 invented a new apparatus for legalised gambling, the off-course betting office, and yet over almost a quarter of a century failed to monitor its impact on individual customers. There are therefore no data on those who 'fall off' or on the social costs of such accidents. Such an approach seems to be an egregious method of developing the leisure activity of gambling.

References

Adler, J. (1966) Gambling, drugs and alcohol: a note on functional equivalents, *Issues in Criminology*, **2** (1), 111–18.

Adler, N. and **Goleman, D.** (1969) Gambling and alcoholism; symptom substitution and functional equivalents, *Quarterly Journal of Studies on Alcohol*, **30**, 733–6.

American Psychiatric Association (1980) *Diagnostic and Statistical Manual of Mental Disorders* (3rd edn) DSM-III. American Psychiatric Association: Washington, DC.

Anokhin, P. K. (1955) Characteristics of the afferent apparatus of a conditioned reflex and its importance for psychology, *Problems of Psychology*, **6**, 16–38.

Arcuri, A. F. (1979) Illegal gambling; a brief review of law enforcement problems, in Lester, D. (ed.), *Gambling Today*. Thomas: Springfield, Illinois.

Armor, D. J., Polich, J. M. and **Stambul, H. B.** (1978) *Alcoholism and treatment*. Wiley: New York.

Ashton, N. (1979) Gamblers, disturbed or healthy? in Lester, D. (ed.), *Gambling Today*. Thomas: Illinois.

Australian Bureau of Statistics (1981) *Taxation Revenue Australia*, Catalogue 5506.0. Canberra.

Ayllon, T. (1963) Intensive treatment of psychotic behaviour by stimulus satiation and food reinforcement, *Behaviour Research and Therapy*, **1**, 53–62.

Bandura, A. (1977) Self-efficacy: toward a unifying theory of behavioural change, *Psychological Review*, **84** (2), 191–215.

Bannister, G. (1977) Cognitive behaviour therapy in a case of compulsive gambler, *Cognitive Therapy and Research*, **13**, 223–7.

Barker, J. C. and **Miller, M.** (1966a) Aversion therapy for compulsive gambling, *Lancet*, i. 491–2.

Barker, J. C. and **Miller, M.** (1966b) Aversion therapy for compulsive gambling, *British Medical Journal*, **2**, 115.

Barker, J. C. and **Miller, M** (1968) Aversion therapy for compulsive gambling, *Journal of Nervous and Mental Diseases*, **146**, 285–302.

Bergin, A. E. (1971) The evaluation of therapeutic outcomes, in Bergin, A. E. and Garfield, S. L. (eds), *Handbook of Psychotherapy and Behavior Change*. Wiley: New York.

Bergler, E. (1957) *The Psychology of Gambling*. Hill and Wang Inc.: New York.

Berlyne, D. E. (1967) Arousal and reinforcement, in Levine, D. (ed.), *Nebraska Symposium on Motivation*. University of Nebraska Press.

Best, J. A., Owen, L. E. and **Trentadue, L.** (1978) Comparison of satiation and rapid smoking, *Addictive Behaviours*, **3**, 71–8.

Blaszczynski, A. (1982) *Personal Communication*. Canberra, Australia.

Blaszczynski, A. P., McConaghy, N., Armstrong, M. S. and **Allcock, C.** (1982) The behavioural treatment of compulsive gamblers. Paper presented at the Fifth National Conference on Behaviour Modification. Brisbane, Australia.

Bolen, D. W. (1974) Gambling: historical highlights, trends, and their implications for contemporary society. Paper presented at the First Annual Conference on Gambling, Las Vegas.

Bolen, D. W. and **Boyd, W. H.** (1968) Gambling and the gambler, *Archives of General Psychiatry*, **18**, 617–30.

British Medical Journal (1968) Editorial on compulsive bling, **2** (2), 69.

Brown, I. (1973) Unpublished report to the Consultation on Compulsive Gambling, London.

Butler, R. A. (1959) Speech on the Second Reading on the Betting and Gaming Act 1960 by the Home Secretary, Official Report, 16 Nov., Col. 812, Hansard.

Caddy, G. R., Addington, H. J. and **Perkins, D.** (1978) Individualised behaviour therapy for alcoholics: a third year independent double-blind follow-up, *Behaviour Research and Therapy*, **16**, 345–62.

Caldwell, G. T. (1972) Leisure co-operatives: the institutionalization of gambling and the growth of large leisure organisation in New South Wales. Unpublished Ph.D. thesis: Australian National University, Canberra.

Callois, R. (1962) *Man, Play and Games*. Thames & Hudson: London.

Campbell, D. P. (1976) Who wants to be a professional gambler? in Eadington, W. R. (ed.), *Gambling and Society: Interdisciplinary Studies on the Subject of Gambling*. Thomas: Springfield, Illinois.

Campbell, F. (1976) Gambling: a positive view, in Eadington, W. R. (ed.), *Gambling and Society: Interdisciplinary Studies on the Subject of Gambling*. Thomas: Springfield, Illinois.

Chaney, E. E., O'Leary, M. R. and **Marlatt, G. A.** (1978) Skill training with alcoholics, *Journal of Consulting and Clinical Psychology*, **46**, 1092–1104.

Clark, W. (1966) Operational definitions of drinking problems and associated prevalence ratios, *Quarterly Journal of Studies on Alcohol*, **27**, 648–68.

Cohen, J. (1972) *Psychological Probability or the Art of Doubt*. Allen & Unwin: London.

Cole, E. W. (ed.) (1908) *Racing Maxims and Methods of Pittsburgh Phil.* (Reprinted 1968), Gamblers Book Club: Las Vegas.

Commission on the Review of the National Policy Toward Gambling (1976) *Gambling in America*, Final Report. (Delivered to President Gerald R. Ford, 15 Oct.) US Government Printing Office: Washington, DC.

Cornish, D. B. (1978) *Gambling: a review of the literature and its implications for policy and research*. HMSO: London.

Cotler, S. B. (1971) The use of different behavioral techniques in treating a case of compulsive gambling, *Behaviour Therapy*, **2**, 579–84.

Cummings, C., Gordon, J. R. and **Marlatt, G. A.** (1980) Relapse, prevention and prediction, in Miller W. R. (ed.), *The Addictive Behaviours: Treatment of Alcoholism, Drug Abuse, Smoking and Obesity*. Pergamon: Oxford.

Custer, R. L. (1982) Pathological gambling, in Whitfield, A. (ed.), *Patients with Alcoholism and Other Drug Problems*. Year Book Publishers: New York.

Custer, R. L. and **Custer, L. F.** (1978) Characteristics of the recovering compulsive gambler: a survey of 150 members of

Gamblers Anonymous. Paper presented at the Fourth Annual Conference on Gambling, Nevada.

Dennis, N., Henriques, F. and **Slaughter, C.** (1969) *Coal is our Life: An Analysis of a Yorkshire Mining Community*. Tavistock Publications: New York.

Devereux, E. C. (1968) Gambling, in Sills, D. L. (ed.), *International Encyclopedia of the Social Sciences*, **6**, 53–62. Macmillan and the Free Press: USA.

Dickerson, M. G. (1974) The effect of betting shop experience on gambling behaviour. Unpublished Ph.D. thesis: University of Birmingham.

Dickerson, M. G. (1975) *Gambling: Associated Problems. A Guide for the Helping Agencies*, Report No. 1 Consultation on compulsive gambling: London.

Dickerson, M. G. (1977a) 'Compulsive' gambling as an addiction: dilemmas, *Scottish Medical Journal*, **22**, 251.

Dickerson, M. G. (1977b) The role of the betting shop environment in the training of compulsive gamblers, *Behavioral Psychotherapy*, **1**, 5; 24–9.

Dickerson, M. G. (1979) FI schedules and persistence at gambling in the UK betting office. *Journal of Applied Behavior Analysis*, **12**, 315–23.

Dickerson, M. G. and **Weeks, D.** (1979) Controlled gambling as a therapeutic technique for compulsive gamblers, *Journal of Behavior Therapy and Experimental Psychiatry*, **10**, 139–41.

Downes, D. M., Davies, B. P., David, M. E. and **Stone, P.** (1976) *Gambling, Work and Leisure: A Study across Three Areas*. Routledge & Kegan Paul: London.

Eadington, W. R. (ed.) (1976) *Gambling and Society: Interdisciplinary Studies on the Subject of Gambling*. Thomas: Springfield, Illinois.

Edwards, G., Orford, J., Egert, S., Guthrie, S., Hawker, A., Hensman, C., Mitcheson, M., Oppenheimer, E. and **Taylor, C.** (1977) Alcoholism: A controlled trial of 'treatment' and 'advice', *Journal of Studies on Alcohol*, **38**, 1004–31.

Edwards, W. (1955) The prediction of decisions among bets, *Journal of Experimental Psychology*, **51**, 201–14.

Epstein, S. (1980) The self-concept: a review and the proposal of an integrated theory of personality, in Staub, E. (ed.), *Personality; basic aspects and current research*. Prentice Hall: Englewood Cliffs, NJ.

Feldman, M..P. and **MacCulloch, M. J.** (1971) *Homosexual Behaviour: Therapy and Assessment.* Pergamon: Oxford.

Ferster, C. B. and **Skinner, B. F.** (1957) *Schedules of Reinforcement.* Appleton-Century-Crofts: New York.

Foa, E. B. and **Steketee, G. S.** (1979) Obsessive–compulsives: conceptual issues and treatment interventions, *Progress in Behaviour Modification*, **8**, 1–53.

Freud, S. (1928) Dostoevsky and parricide, in Strachey, J. (ed.), *Collected Papers*, 5. Basic Books: New York.

Galdston, I. (1960) The gambler and his love, *American Journal of Psychiatry*, **117**, 553–5.

Gathercole, C. (1973) Unpublished report to the Consultation on 'Compulsive' Gambling, London.

Geha, R. (1970) Dostoevsky and 'the gambler': a contribution to the psychogenesis of gambling, *Psychoanalytic Review*, **57**, 289–303.

Glen, A., Custer, R. L. and **Burns, R.** (1975) The in-patient treatment of compulsive gamblers. Paper presented at the Second Annual Conference on Gambling, Nevada.

Goffman, E. (1969) *Where the Action Is.* Allen Lane: London.

Goodman, B., Saltzman, M., Edwards, W. and **Krontz, D. H.** (1979) Prediction of bids for two-outcome gambles in a casino setting, *Organisation of Behavior and Human Performance*, **24**, 382–99.

Goorney, A. B. (1968) Treatment of a compulsive horserace gambler by aversion therapy, *British Journal of Psychiatry*, **114**, 329–33.

Greenberg, H. R. (1980) Psychology of gambling, in Kaplan, H. I., Freedman, A. M., and Sadock, B. J. (eds), *Comprehensive Textbook of Psychiatry* 3rd edn. Williams & Wilkins: Baltimore/London.

Greenson, R. (1947) On gambling, *American Image*, **4**, 61.

Halliday, J. and **Fuller, P.** (eds) (1974) *The Psychology of Gambling.* Allen Lane: London.

Hare, R. D. and **Schalling, D.** (eds) (1978) *Psychopathic Behaviour: Approaches to Research.* Wiley: Chichester, England.

Harris, H. I. (1964) Gambling addiction in an adolescent male, *Psychoanalytic Quarterly*, **33**, 515–25.

Havard, J. D. J. (1977) Alcohol and road accidents, in Edwards, G. and Grant, M. (eds), *Alcoholism: New Knowledge and New*

Responses. Croom Helm: London.

Haynes, S. N. and **Wilson, C. C.** (1979) *Behavioural Assessment*. Jossey-Bass: London/Washington.

Henslin, J. M. (1967) Craps and magic, *American Journal of Sociology*, **73** (3), 316–30.

Herman, R. D. (ed.) (1967) *Gambling*. Harper & Row: New York.

Hess, H. F. and **Diller, J. V.** (1969) Motivation for gambling as revealed in the marketing methods of the legitimate gambling industry, *Psychological Reports*, **25**, 19–27.

HMSO (1978) Royal Commission on Gambling: Final Report, (Rothschild Report) London.

Hochauer, B. (1970) Decision-making in roulette, *Acta Psychologica*, **34** (2–3), 357–66.

Hodgson, R., Rankin, H. and **Stockwell, T.** (1979) Alcohol dependence and the priming effect, *Behaviour Research and Therapy*, **17**, 379–87.

Jellinek, E. M. (1952) The phases of alcohol addiction, *Quarterly Journal of Studies on Alcohol*, **13**, 673–84.

Jones, J. P. (1973) *Gambling Yesterday and Today*. David & Charles: Newton Abbot.

Joyce, K. M. (1975) Social aspects of gambling. Submission to Commission on the Review of the National Policy Toward Gambling. US Government Printing Office: Washington, DC.

Kat, B. (1974) personal communication.

Kazdin, A. E. and **Wilson, G. T.** (1978) Criteria for evaluating psychotherapy, *Archives of General Psychiatry*, **35**, 407–18.

Kendell, R. E. (1979) Alcoholism: a medical or a political problem? *British Medical Journal*, i, 367–71.

Knapp, T. J. (1976) A functional analysis of gambling behaviour, in Eadington, W. R. (ed.), *Gambling and Society: Interdisciplinary Studies on the Subject of Gambling*. Thomas: Springfield, Illinois.

Kogan, N. and **Wallach, M. A.** (1967) Risk-taking as a function of the situation, the person and the group, in Newcomb, T. N. (ed.), *New Directions in Psychology* III. Rinehart & Winston: New York.

Koller, K. M. (1972) Treatment of poker-machine addicts by aversion therapy, *Medical Journal of Australia*, i, 742–5.

Kroeber, A. (1948) *Anthropology: Race, Language, Culture,*

Psychology, Prehistory. Harcourt Brace: New York.

Kusyszyn, I. (1972) The gambling addict versus the gambling professional, *International Journal of Addictions*, **7** (2), 387–93.

Kusyszyn, I. (1973) The Psychology of Gambling. Invited address, Annual meeting of the Rocky Mountain Psychological Association, Las Vegas.

Kusyszyn, I. and **Kallai, C.** (1975) The gambling person, healthy or sick? Paper presented at the meeting of the Second Annual Conference on Gambling, Nevada.

Kusyszyn, I. and **Rutter, R.** (1978) Personality characteristics of heavy, light, non-gamblers and lottery players. Paper presented at the meeting of the Fourth Annual Conference on Gambling, Nevada.

Ladouceur, R. and **Mayraud, M.** (1981) The evaluation of the 'illusion of control': type of feedback, outcome sequence and number of trials. Paper presented at the Fifth National Conference on Gambling and Risk Taking, Lake Tahoe, USA.

Langer, E. J. (1975) The illusion of control, *Journal of Personality and Social Psychology*, **32** (2), 311–28.

Langer, E. J. and **Roth, J.** (1975) Heads I win, tails it's chance: the illusion of control as a function of the sequence of outcomes in a purely chance task, *Journal of Personality and Social Psychology*, **32** (6), 951–5.

Lefcourt, H. M. (1980) Locus of control and coping with life's events, in Staub, E. (ed.), *Personality; Basic Aspects and Current Research*. Prentice Hall: Englewood Cliffs, NJ.

Lesieur, H. R. (1979) The compulsive gambler's spiral of options and involvement, *Psychiatry*, **42** (1), 79–87.

Lester, D. (ed.) (1979) *Gambling Today*. Thomas: Springfield, Illinois.

Levitz, L. S. (1971) The experimental induction of compulsive gambling behaviours, *Dissertation Abstracts International*, **32**, B, 1216–17.

Lewis, A. J. (1936) Problems of obsessional illness, *Proceedings of the Royal Society of Medicine*, **29**, 325.

Lewis, D. J. and **Duncan, C. P.** (1956) Effect of different percentages of money reward on extinction of a lever-pulling response, *Journal of Experimental Psychology*, **52**, 23–7.

Lewis, D. J. and **Duncan, C. P.** (1957) Expectation and resistance to extinction of a lever-pulling response as functions of percentage of reinforcement and amount of reward, *Journal of Experimental Psychology*, **54**, 115–20.

Lewis, D. J. and Duncan, C. P. (1958) Expectation and resistance to extinction of a lever-pulling response as a function of percentage of reinforcement and number of acquisition trials, *Journal of Experimental Psychology*, **55**, 121–8.

Lindner, R. M. (1950) The psychodynamics of gambling, *Annuals of the American Academy of Political and Social Science*, **269**, 93.

Ling, T. N. and Buckman, J. (1963) *Lysergic Acid and Ritalin in the Treatment of Neuroses.* Lombard Press: London.

Logan, F. A. (1979) Hybrid theory of operant conditioning, *Psychological Review*, **86**, 507–41.

Luria, A. (1961) *The Role of Speech in the Regulation of Normal and Abnormal Behaviors.* Liveright: New York.

Luria, A. (1969) Speech and formation of mental processes, in Cole, M., Maltzman, I. (eds), *A Handbook of Contemporary Soviet Psychology.* Basic Books: New York.

Malkin, D. (1981) An empirical investigation into some aspects of problem gambling. Unpublished Masters thesis: University of Western Australia.

Marlatt, G. A. (1979) Alcohol use and problem drinking: a cognitive-behavioural analysis, in Kendall, P.. C., and Hollon, S. D. (eds), *Cognitive Behavioural Interventions, Theory, Research and Procedures.* Academic Press: London.

Matussek, P. (1953) On the psychodynamics of the gambler, *Journal of Psychology and Psychotherapy*, **1**, 232.

McConaghy, N. (1969) Subjective and penile plethysmograph responses following aversion-relief and apomorphine therapy for homosexual impulses, *British Journal of Psychiatry*, **115**, 723–30.

McConaghy, N. (1970) Subjective and penile plethysmograph responses to aversion therapy for homosexuality: a follow-up study, *British Journal of Psychiatry*, **117**, 555–60.

McConaghy, N. (1980) Behaviour completion mechanisms rather than primary drives maintain behavioural patterns. *Activitas Nervosa Superior (Praha)*, **22** (2), 138–51.

McConaghy, N., Proctor, D. and Barr, R. (1972) Subjective and penile plethysmography responses to aversion therapy for homosexuality: a partial replication, *Archives of Sexual Behaviour*, **2**, 65–78.

McConaghy, N., Armstrong, M. S., Blaszcynski, A. and Allcock, C. (1982) The mode of action of behaviour therapies in compulsive activities. Unpublished manuscript.

McGlothin, W. H. (1954) A psychometric study of gambling, *Journal of Consulting Psychology*, **18**, 145–9.

McPherson, D. and Sutton, A. (1981) *Reconstructing Psychological Practice*. Croom Helm: London.

Meichenbaum, D. and Asarnow, J. (1979) Cognitive-behavioural modification and metacognitive development: implications for the classroom, in Kendall, P. C., Hollon, S. D. (eds), *Cognitive-Behavioural Interventions*. Academic Press: London New York.

Miller, W. R. (ed.) (1980) *The Addictive Behaviours: Treatment of Alcoholism, Drug Abuse, Smoking and Obesity*. Pergamon: Oxford.

Montgomery, H. R. and Kreitzer, S. (1968) 'Compulsive' gambling and behaviour therapy. Paper presented at the California State Psychological Association Convention, Santa Barbara, California.

Moody, G. E. (1972) *The Facts about the 'Money Factories'*. Churches Council on Gambling: London.

Moran, E. (1970a) Varieties of pathological gambling, *British Journal of Psychiatry*, **116** (535), 593–7.

Moran, E. (1970b) Gambling as a form of dependence, *British Journal of Addiction*, **64**, 419–28.

Moran, E. (1970c) Clinical and social aspects of risk-taking, *Proceedings of the Royal Society of Medicine*, **63**, 1273–7.

Moran, E. (1975) Pathological gambling, in *British Journal of Psychiatry*, Special Publication No. 9: *Contemporary Psychiatry*, Royal College of Psychiatrists: London.

Moran, E. (1975a) Book reviews, *British Journal of Psychiatry*, 127, 297.

Moran, E. (1979) An assessment of the Report of the Royal Commission on Gambling, 1976–1978, *British Journal of Addiction*, **74**, 3–9.

Moravec, J. D. (1980) Professional response to the pathological gambler: the Miami experience. Paper presented at the American Psychological Association Meeting, Montreal.

Moskowitz, J. A. (1980) Lithium and lady luck, *New York State Journal of Medicine*, **80**, 785–8.

Mowrer, O. H. (1960) *Learning Theory and the Symbolic Processes*. Wiley: New York.

Murray, H. A. (1938) *Explorations in Personality*. Science Editions: (Reprinted 1962), New York.

Myers, I. B. (1962) *The Myers-Brigg Type Indicator Manual*. Educational Testing Service: Princeton, New Jersey.

Newman, O. (1972) *Gambling: Hazard and Reward*. Athlone Press: London.

Oldman, D. J. (1974) Chance and skill: a study of roulette, *Sociology*, **8**, 407–26.

Oldman, D. J. (1978) Compulsive gamblers, *Sociological Review*, **26**, 349–71.

Orford, J. (1974) personal communication.

Patisson, E. M., Sobell, M. B. and **Sobell, L. C.** (1977), *Emerging Concepts of Alcohol Dependence*. Springer: New York.

Pechacek, T. F. and **Danaher, B. G.** (1979) How and why people quit smoking: a cognitive-behavioural analysis, in Kendall, P. C., Hollon, S. D. (ed), *Cognitive-Behavioural Interventions*. Academic Press: London/New York.

Peck, D. F. (1973) *The modification of habitual gambling behaviour*. European Association for Behaviour Therapy and Modification. Urban & Schwarzenberg: Munich.

Peck, D. F. and **Ashcroft, J. B** (1972) The use of stimulus satiation in the modification of habitual gambling. *Proceedings of the Second British and European Association Conference on Behaviour Modification*, Kilkenny, Ireland.

Perkins, E. B. (1950) *Gambling in English Life*. Epworth Press: London.

Pokorny, M. R. (1972) Compulsive gambling and the family, *British Journal of Medical Psychology*, **45** (4), 355–64.

Politzer, R. M. and **Morrow, J. S.** (1980) The Johns Hopkins University Compulsive Gambling Counselling Centre. Paper presented at the American Psychological Association Annual Meeting, Sept.

Politzer, R. M., Morrow, J. S. and **Leavey, S. B.** (1981) Report on the societal cost of pathological gambling and the cost-benefit/effectiveness of treatment. Paper presented at Fifth Annual Conference on Gambling and Risk Taking, Lake Tahol, USA.

Popper, K. R. (1963) *Conjectures and Refutations*. Routledge and Kegan Paul: London.

Pruitt, D. G. and **Kimmel, M. J.** (1977) Twenty years of experimental gaming: critique, synthesis, and suggestions for the future, *Annual Review of Psychology*, **28**, 363–92.

Rachman, S. and **Hodgson, R.** (1980) *Obsessions and Compulsions*. Prentice-Hall: Englewood Cliffs, NJ.

Rachman, S. and **Teasdale, J.** (1969) *Aversion Therapy and Behaviour Disorders: An Analysis*. Routledge & Kegan Paul: London.

Rachman, S. and **Wilson, G. T.** (1980) *The Effects of Psychological Therapy*. Pergamon Press: Oxford.

Rankin, H. Hodgson, R. and **Stockwell, T.** (1979) The concept of craving and its measurement, *Behaviour Research and Therapy*, **17**, 389–96.

Rice, C. (1969) *Nick the Greek : King of the Gamblers*. Funk & Wagnalls: New York.

Richardson, A. (1968) A shipboard study of some British born immigrants returning to the United Kingdom from Australia, *International Migration*, 6, 221–34.

Rimm, D. C. and **Masters, J. C.** (1979) *Behaviour Therapy*. Academic Press: London.

Roman, P. M. (1980) Alternatives to the medicalisation of deviant behaviour, *Psychiatry*, **43**, 168–74.

Rotter, J. B. (1975) Some problems and misconceptions related to the construct of internal versus external control of reinforcement, *Journal of Consulting and Clinical Psychology*, **43**, 56–67.

Rule, B. G. and **Fischer, D. G.** (1970) Impulsivity, subjective probability, cardiac response and risk-taking: correlates and factors, *Personality*, **1** (3), 251–60.

Rule, B. G., Nutter, R. W. and **Fischer, D. G.** (1971) The effect of arousal on risk-taking, *Personality*, **2** (3), 239–47.

Sarason, S. B., Carroll, C. F., Maton, K., Cohen, S. and **Lorentz, E.** (1977) *Human Services and Resource Networks*. Jossey-Bass: London/Washington.

Saunders , D. M. and **Wookey, P. E.** (1978) Behavioural analyses of gambling. Paper presented to the British Psychological Society Conference, London.

Scarne, J. (1975) *Scarne's New Complete Guide to Gambling*. Constable: London.

Schacht, T. and **Nathan, P. E.** (1977) But is it good for the psychologists? Appraisal and status of DSM-III, *American Psy-*

chologist, **32**, 1017–25.

Schmidt, W. (1977) Cirrhosis and alcohol consumption: an epidemiological perspective, in Edwards, G., Grant, M. (eds), *Alcoholism: New Knowledge and New Responses*. Croom Helm: London.

Scodel, A. (1964) Inspirational group therapy: a study of Gamblers Anonymous, *American Journal of Psycho-therapy*, **18** (1), 115–25.

Seager, C. P. (1970) Treatment of compulsive gamblers using electrical aversion, *British Journal of Psychiatry*, **117**, 545–53.

Seager, C. P., Pokorny, M. R. and **Black, D.** (1966) Aversion therapy for compulsive gambling, *Lancet*, i, 546.

Skinner, B. F. (1953) *Science and Human Behaviour*. Free Press: New York.

Skinner, B. F. (1972) *Beyond Freedom and Dignity?* Cape: London.

Skolnick, J. H. (1978) *House of Cards*. Little, Brown & Co.: Boston.

Smith, S. and **Razzell, P.** (1975) *The Pools Winners*. Caliban Books: London.

Sobell, M. B. and **Sobell, L. C.** (1978) *Behavioral Treatment of Alcohol Problems*. Plenum: New York.

Spielberger, C. D., Gorsuch, R. L. and **Lushene, R.** (1970) *Manual for the State-Trait Anxiety Inventory (Self-Evaluation Questionnaire)*. Consulting Psychologist Press: Palo Alto, California.

Spitzer, R. L. and **Williams, J. B. W.** (1980) Classification of mental disorders and DSM-III, in Kaplan, H. I., Freedman, A. M. and Williams, J. B. W. (eds), *Comprehensive Textbook of Psychiatry* III. Williams & Wilkins: Baltimore/London.

Strictland, L. H., Lewicki, R. J. and **Katz, A. M.** (1966) Temporal orientation and perceived control as determinants of risk-taking, *Journal of Experimental Social Psychology*, **2**, 143–51.

Szasz, T. S. (1961) *The Myth of Mental Illness*. Hoeber: New York.

Taber, J. I. (1979) Memorandum to Public Health and Welfare Committee, The Senate of the State of Pennsylvania, subject: Testimony on Senate Bill No. 909, dealing with the treatment of compulsive gamblers, 28, Nov.

Tec. N. (1964) *Gambling in Sweden*. Bedminster Press: NJ.

Thomas, W. I. (1901) The gaming instinct, *American Journal of Sociology*, **6**, 750–63.

Thorp, E. (1966) *Beat the Dealer*. Random House: New York.

Trute, B. and **Loewen, A.** (1978) Public attitude toward the mentally ill as a function of prior personal experience, *Social Psychiatry*, **13**, 79–84.

Uston, K. and **Rapoport, R.** (1977) *The Big Player*. Holt, Rinehart & Winston: New York.

Victor, R. G. and **Krug, C. M.** (1967) Paradoxical intention in the treatment of compulsive gambling, *American Journal of Psycho-Therapy*, **21** (4), 808–14.

Von Hattingberg, H. (1914) Analerotik, angstlust und eigensinn, *Internationale Zeitschrift für Psycholanalyse*, **2**, 244–58.

Vygotsky, L. (1962) *Thought and Language*. Wiley: New York.

Weinstein, D. and **Deitch, L.** (1974) *The Impact of Legalised Gambling. The Socioeconomic Consequences of Lotteries and Off-Track Betting*. Praeger: New York.

Wong, G. (1980) The obsessional aspects of compulsive gambling. Paper presented to the Society for the Study of Gambling, London.

Wray, I. (1980) A retrospective survey of Gamblers Anonymous. Unpublished M.Phil. thesis: University of Edinburgh.

Wray, I. and **Dickerson, M. G.** (1981) Cessation of high-frequency gambling and 'withdrawal' symptoms, *British Journal of Addiction*, **76**, 401–5.

Zola, I. K. (1964) Observations on gambling in a lower-class setting, in Becker, H. S. (ed.), *The Other Side, Perspectives on Deviance*. Free Press: Illinois.

Zuckerman, M. (1971) Dimensions of sensation seeking, *Journal of Consulting and Clinical Psychology*, **36**, 45–52.

Zuckerman, M. (1979) Sensation seeking and risk-taking, in Izard, C. E. (ed.), *Emotions in Personality and Psychopathology*. Plenum: New York.

Zuckerman, M., Eysenck, S. B. G. and **Eysenck, H. J.** (1978) Sensation seeking in England and America: cross-cultural, age and sex comparisons, *Journal of Consulting and Clinical Psychology*, **46**, 139–49.

Index